DEAF
TO
EVIDENCE

PETER JACKSON

The right of Peter Jackson to be identified as the author of this work has been asserted by him in accordance with the Copyright, Designs and Patents Act 1988

Published by Cox & Jackson

© Peter Jackson 1998

ISBN 0-9532206-1-3

Printed in Great Britain

Contents

Acknowledgements		5
1.	Introduction	7
2.	Guilty by Reason of Deafness	9
3.	The Case of the Bloody Footprint	13
4.	Hanged, but was he Innocent?	32
5.	A Blemish on Justice	50
6.	The Long Arrest	119

Photograph Acknowledgements	135
Research & Bibliography	137

To My Wife, Maureen

Acknowledgements

A book like this could never be published without the assistance and encouragement of many others.

My thanks go to my wife, Maureen, for her assistance in researching some of the material; to Nancy Cox and Cheridah Sword for their assistance in telephone interpreting with various persons overseas.

I thank also the staff of Jackson District Library, Michigan, USA for their assistance in locating material in connection with one of the stories.

I thank Catherine White, Sheila and Teddy Webb and other anonymous persons in New Zealand for their contributions to that particular story.

I am grateful also to the staff of the *West Australian* newspaper, and to other anonymous persons for their assistance with the main story in this book.

Thanks are also due to Terence O'Hara for making a reproduction shoe. He would say it was an interesting challenge.

I also thank Magazine Design & Publishing Ltd. for permission to reproduce one of their photographs.

1 :   Introduction

It is said that murder excites the public imagination like no other crime and encourages the amateur sleuth in all of us. If this is true, then the amateur lawyer in all of us is also encouraged to fight for the innocence of those unfortunate to fall foul of any process of criminal law which they are powerless to fight themselves.
This is especially true for those who have problems in communication which create barriers in their attempts to prove their innocence of any wrongdoing.
The title of this book comes from the popular saying: *There's none so blind as those that see, and none so deaf as those that hear*, and covers I think the circumstances of the five cases described in the book.
It can be no satisfaction to anybody that one man was denied a fair trial, that two men spent 20 years and 10 years respectively in jail for murders they did not commit, that one man was unjustly hanged, or that another had to wait nearly two years in jail on remand without bail only to be acquitted when the case eventually came to trial because it was found the police had bungled the original investigation.
I believe that these cases are just the tip of an iceberg.
All the cases in this book have been taken from countries where English is the main spoken language, but it would be true to say that because of difficulties of access and language differences, it has not been possible for the author to investigate miscarriages of justice that occurred in non-English speaking countries.
The British university of Durham recently published a book *"Equality Before the Law - Deaf people's access to justice"* which chronicled research into a number of court cases in England, Wales and Scotland where clearly

access to justice gave raise to grave concerns as to whether such access was in fact accessible. It concentrated on the adequacy and accessibility of sign language interpreting provision in police interrogations and in courts. This research should be of interest to all directly concerned with the process of the law and civil rights.

For two individuals in this book at least, the publication of this research comes too late.

Peter W. Jackson
October 1998

2.   1904 : Stafford, England

GUILTY BY REASON OF DEAFNESS

It was not a murder. It was not even a very serious crime. It was only the theft of a few shillings. Even then, the crime was not proven and the man accused of the crime had denied the theft, protesting his innocence saying he could prove he had not done the theft.

Yet the full weight of the law ensured that the poor man was to be treated very harshly, spending many years in prison, with little chance to prove his innocence, making a mockery of the principle that every person was to be judged innocent of any crime until proven guilty.

At the turn of the 20th Century, England and Wales were still subject to the provisions of the Criminal Lunatics Act, 1800 (commonly referred to by justices as "the stat. 39 & 40, Geo.3, c.94, S.2") on how persons accused of crimes, and judged to be insane, were treated by the courts. Following a ruling by Mr. Justice Parke in the case of *Rex. v. Dyson* in 1831, Deaf persons accused of crimes were also subject to the Criminal Lunatics Act and had to have a jury impannelled to decide whether they were mute by malice or by the visitation of God. If, as it always was, the finding was by visitation by God, the jury were then sworn a second time to decide if the accused was able to plead to the indictment and to understand the proceedings of the court by reason of his inability to communicate with or be communicated with by others.

Frequently, it was found that the Deaf person was unable to plead to the indictment or understand the proceedings, whereupon the sitting justice would order that the accused be detained in prison or a criminal asylum "until His or Her Majesty's pleasure be known".

For many Deaf persons, this meant being confined to a prison or a criminal asylum for many years, or even for life, without the chance of a proper trial.

So, in 1904 in rural Staffordshire, when a Deaf labourer named Frederick Emery who was unable to read or write was arrested for the theft of a few shillings despite his protests of innocence (in sign language) and arraigned before Staffordshire Assizes, his trial followed the normal pattern of events for that time, and he was found to be non-sane by reason of his inability to communicate with or be communicated with by others, and ordered to be detained until His Majesty's pleasure be known.

The move so incensed his friends, both Deaf and hearing, neighbours and family that they campaigned for his release but the process of the law moves slowly, and Frederick Emery languished in prison for five long years before a writ of *habeas corpus* was successfully granted by the courts.

The case came up before Staffordshire Assizes on 23rd March 1909 before Lord Chief Justice Alverstone, and Lord Justices Darling and Jelf, when they had to decide upon a rule *nisi* to the Governor of his Majesty's Prison at Stafford to show cause why a writ of *habeas corpus* should not be issued direct to him to have the body of the applicant Frederick Emery produced before the court to undergo and receive a proper trial.

Emery's solicitor, S.R.C.Bosanquet, argued before the court that unfitness to plead arising from an inability to communicate with others was not insanity, and that there had to be a mental defect and a finding to that effect before a prisoner could be detained as a criminal lunatic. He argued that Frederick Emery could communicate by reason of sign language, that he was not mentally defective within the meaning of the Lunatics Act, and that if the trial was conducted in sign language through the medium of an interpreter as had happened in several instances, the prisoner might obtain a fair trial, and be able to prove his innocence of the charges arraigned against him.

Lord Chief Justice Alverstone stated that he was glad that this matter had come up before the court "because it enables us to re-declare what the position of the matter is."

"It is perfectly true," he said, "as Mr.Bosanquet pointed out, that the words 'inability to plead', 'inability to understand', 'inability to communicate with any person' are not mentioned in the statute (the Criminal Lunatics Act). The only words mentioned are 'shall be insane, and shall be upon arraignment found to be so by a jury so that a person cannot be tried upon such an indictment'. We are being asked to say that a previous decision of the Court for Crown Cases reserved on this point is not binding upon us. It is perfectly true that a decision of the judges on assizes would not be binding upon us. At the same time, I would be unwilling to upset the practice established by many experienced judges for almost a century."

He found that there was not the slightest ground for Frederick Emery to be released from the sentence imposed upon him, and that the order for his detention was perfectly proper.

His colleagues on the bench, Justices Darling and Jelf, supported this view, and the unfortunate Frederick Emery was returned to Stafford Prison still without having had the opportunity to prove his innocence.

Not until 1953 (by coincidence, also 23rd March) was this practice of ordering the detention of Deaf people to be held until his/her Majesty's pleasure be known without a fair trial stopped, when in an historic decision, Mr. Justice Delvin (later to be England's Lord Chief Justice) stated, "It cannot be our law that by some formality of procedure, counsel for the defence should be prevented from being able to submit evidence his client did not commit the crime before a jury and so achieving, if he can, a verdict of Not Guilty."

It was too late, of course, for Frederick Emery and doubtless countless other Deaf people like him.

It is not known what happened to Frederick Emery after he was returned to Stafford Prison, but in 1915, he was still there.

3.   1914 : Jackson, Michigan, USA.

THE CASE OF THE BLOODY FOOTPRINT

Spring Arbor was, in the early 1900's, a small farming community approximately ten miles south-west of the city of Jackson in Michigan. Many of its inhabitants had grown up together on the farms, some even being born and living all their lives on the same farm. Consequently, many knew each other and as good neighbours would do, would help out on each other's farms if any help was needed.

Seventeen-year-old Arthur White was one such good neighbour. He lived with another young man named Elmer Lehr and was in the habit of going to the Srycock Farm about a mile and half from where he lived a few times a week to help to cut logs and carry coal into the house of the elderly woman who lived alone on the 40-acre farm.

On Friday evening the 27th February 1914, when the young man went out to the Srycock Farm, it was to be his first visit since the preceding Sunday as he had been laid low with a severe illness.

When he arrived there at 7.30 p.m., he found the place in darkness which was unusual for Mrs.Srycock. Feeling a bit anxious, he felt his way into the farmhouse which was unheated despite the snow that lay on the ground outside until he managed to find an oil lamp and light it. Only then did he see the state of the farmhouse - it had been ransacked and the floor was covered with discarded belongings and other debris, including pools of blood.

On the kitchen table, there was evidence of a half-eaten supper.

"Mrs. Srycock! Where are you?" he called out anxiously.

Receiving no reply, he spotted a trial through the pools of blood leading from the back of the stove towards a small bedroom at the rear of the kitchen, and there, he discovered the body of the elderly woman.

The body lay half on the bed and half on the floor of the bedroom, with the head on the blood-soaked mattress covered by an apron. Lifting this off the dead woman, Arthur White saw that she had been shot, and decided that he had better contact the sheriff's department.

Leaving the farmhouse, White hurried across the snowbound fields towards the next farm, where lived a farmer named Albert Worth, and told him what he had discovered. Immediately, Worth communicated the news to the Sheriff's office in Jackson City before going over to the Srycock farm to see for himself.

The call in Jackson City was received by Deputy Sheriff Holland, who quickly rounded up one of the district coroners, W.J.Marks, and travelled out the ten miles fro Jackson in one of the few newly-fangled automobiles to be found in the district.

By the time the deputy and the coroner arrived out at the death scene, many of the local farmers had been at the house trampling through, and disturbing evidence.

Asking everyone to leave the premises, the deputy waited for the arrival of Sheriff Strobel and other deputies whilst Coroner Marks went in to examine the body, which was identified as that of Catherine Srycock, a 75-year-old widow who lived alone at the farm as a semi-recluse. The coroner confirmed that the victim had been shot, and was dead.

Coroner Marks noted that the dead woman's cat, which lived with her, was sitting beside the bed as if standing vigil.

Examining the crime scene, the police officers surmised that Mrs.Srycock had been seated at her kitchen table eating supper when she was interrupted by an intruder, for there were half-eaten scraps of food on the plate, and a half-full cup of cold tea remained untouched beside the plate of food.

The intruder had evidently crept up to the aged woman when she was eating and had fired at her as she sat at her table, and she had leaped up and staggered behind the stove to escape her murderer, for there were splatters of blood beside where the chair had fallen over. The woman had then fallen, and her assailant had stood over her prostrate form and fired several more bullets into her head.

Judging by the trails of blood, the murderer had then searched the body of the woman for any valuables, then he had dragged her by the feet, head downward on the floor, to the bed and had hurled the body onto the bed. The body had, however, partially rolled off the bed so that the victim's head remained on the mattress whilst the lower half of the body rested on the floor. There, the killer had left the body and proceeded to search the house.

He had rifled the bureau and dresser drawers in a search for money and valuables; the contents of the bureau drawers were dumped onto the floor and kicked about by the murderer. He had found the old woman's pocket-book and turned it inside out before throwing it down onto the floor to join the other dumped items. The murderer had evidently not found much money, thus disproving the theory held by some local people that the old woman kept hidden in her house large sums of money.

The police also found that the pools of blood had not yet become completely dry, and that rigor mortis had not yet set in upon the arrival of Deputy Sheriff Holland and

Coroner Marks. Police officers were thoroughly convinced that the dead woman had been slain on Thursday night, and the evidence of the half-eaten supper tended to support that theory.

Catherine Srycock, the victim, had been born in the same farmhouse, and had lived there all her life. A widow for many years, she had lived with her brother until his death in late 1912 and afterwards on her own. She was so badly afflicted by rheumatism to such an extent that she could only move about her house by pushing her chair in front of her. She had since the death of her brother also exhibited signs of senile dementia which led her to be unable to look after her own affairs, and a guardian was legally appointed to manage the farm for her and take charge of her affairs.

Police officers arranged for the body to be transported for an autopsy to the Knickerbocker undertaking rooms in Jackson, then sealed up the house. At this stage, the police did not have any clues as to who the killer might be, but they established the old woman had last been seen by 15-year-old Edna Pardee on Thursday afternoon. The young Miss Pardee was the daughter of a Fenn Pardee, a farmer who lived in the next farm to Catherine Srycock. It was Fenn Pardee who had been legally appointed guardian by Jackson County District Court to manage Mrs. Srycock's affairs and her farm. He paid her an allowance of $25 per month and managed the farmstead on her behalf.

Just recently, an unsuccessful attempt had been made to remove Fenn Pardee as the guardian, and there was a theory that someone had thought Mr.Pardee had turned over to the dead woman all the money she owned whilst the attempt to remove him as guardian took place.

A distant relative, Lloyd Wilson who was heir to the property, had applied to replace Fenn Pardee as Mrs.Srycock's guardian but had been unable to furnish the necessary bond and the court had rejected his application as appointed guardian. He had been bitter about this, and had not been seen in the district since January 15th, and because of this, police officers considered him as a possible suspect in the killing.

For the moment, police arrested Arthur White on suspicion of the murder, but his story checked out and he was released after a night spent in the cells.

Meanwhile, back at the Knickerbocker undertaking rooms, an autopsy was performed on the Saturday afternoon by Dr. W.A.Stoops, witnessed by Coroner Morrison.

The autopsy disclosed that Mrs.Srycock has four bullets fired at her. The first bullet was made whilst she was standing, presumably to get away from her assailant, as it had entered the back of her skull and passed right through her head, exiting at the front. The other three bullets had been fired into her body as she lay on the floor.

All four bullets were determined to have been fired from a powerful .32 calibre revolver, of which no trace was found at the murder scene.

Police officers at the murder scene were especially interested in sleigh and hoof marks evident in the snow outside the farmhouse which had not been made by any person who had been at the farm during the discovery of the murder.

Further questioning of neighbours revealed that a young man aged 20 had been seen in the vicinity of the farm on the Thursday evening. As the young man in question had previously been involved in some unsavoury petty crime and was known to the police as one with a bit of a reputation in the community, He was also known to be a regular visitor to the Srycock Farm looking for odd-jobs.

Police traced the young man to a pool room in East Coutland Street in Jackson on the Saturday evening and placed him under arrest. The following afternoon, he was taken in handcuffs by Deputies Welch and Holland, and shown the body of the dead woman at the Knickerbocker undertaking rooms.

"How could anybody do an awful thing like that? She was a very good friend to me," he was reported to have told the deputies.

On the Monday following the murder, police revealed that they had arrested and were holding in custody one Harold Winney, aged 20, whose address was given as the Adams hotel at the Y.M.C.A., Jackson.

Sheriff Strobel informed newspaper reporters that Winney would be arraigned in court that day charged with breaking and entering into the Finch and Bower hardware store. He stated that two .32 revolvers identified as items stolen from the hardware store had been found in Winney's possession at the time of his arrest. He said that the arrested man had denied the murder of Catherine Srycock, but the fact that one of the .32 revolvers had been fired very recently was very suggestive of his involvement in the crime.

The sheriff told reporters that Winney had positively been identified by store assistants as the man who had examined the same .32 calibre revolvers during a visit to the store on the Wednesday afternoon of the preceding week, prior to the burglary of the store on Wednesday night, 25 February, when the revolvers plus an undisclosed sum of money were stolen from the store.

He added that police officers were also trying to pin upon Winney a charge of stealing a horse and cutter rig from a site on Jackson and Main Streets on Thursday evening. The horse and rig were found abandoned early Friday morning hitched on West Wesley Street.

Police had traced movements of the horse and rig, which was fitted with sleigh poles, out to Greenwood Avenue to a point close to the direction where the Srycock Farm lay, and they had two witnesses who could place the horse and rig near the murder scene. The horse rig was unusual in that it had been fitted with harness bells which emitted a peculiar sound which could only be heard by someone possessing normal hearing facilities, and the two witnesses had identified those sounds made by the horse and rig without being able to state who was driving the rig that night.

This was another important factor in the arrest of Harold Winney for he was completely deaf, therefore he would not have realised that the horse had harness bells that identified its movements wherever it went. Not only was he completely deaf, he was also handicapped since birth by one leg which was about nine inches shorter than the other. To enable him to walk, he wore an iron stirrup fitted to his right boot or shoe.

Although he could not hear, Winney possessed excellent speech and could talk, and talk he did. From the start, he flatly denied that he had committed the murder and that he did not know anything about it other than what he had been told by people in Jackson.

The sheriff added that his officers were having a hard time interrogating Winney because of his deafness. Winney could not lip-read well, and everything that was said to him had to be written down, though Winney answered each question verbally. The investigation was continuing and the police would be looking for more evidence to collaborate what they had on Winney.

It was certainly a busy period for the Jackson county police. Not only did they have the Srycock murder and the Finch & Bower hardware store robbery, they had also just arrested an armed train robber named Leo Costlow, alias Harry Warner, who had held up a Pullman sleeping car on a Michigan central passenger train a few miles west of Jackson on January 23rd. They had put Costlow in the same cell as Winney - this was to have some repercussions for Winney.

As part of their ongoing investigation to gather more evidence against Winney, sheriff's deputies returned to the Srycock Farm for a more detailed examination on Tuesday 3rd March, five days after the discovery of the body, and over 40 hours since the arrest of Harold Winney at the New York pool room in Jackson.

The Srycock Farm was still sealed up, as it had been by the police after removal of the body on Friday for the autopsy, and no police officers had since been back to the farmhouse. The contents of the farmhouse had not been disturbed or cleaned up, and the splashes of blood were still there on the kitchen and bedroom floors.

"Look at this!"

One of the police officers was pointing to a footprint in the blood.

"Why, that's a print of Harold Winney's iron shoe," another policeman exclaimed in excitement.

The blood had dried and the impression was sharply defined. They went and got Winney's shoe, and compared it with the print in the blood. It was a perfect fit. There was no question about it being the murderer's footprint, and only Harold Winney could have made it. To police officers, they were absolutely certain they had the right man and Winney was as good as convicted.

Nonetheless, that footprint bothered the sheriff when he and the prosecutor, District Attorney Rossman, were called out to the Srycock Farm and had the opportunity to examine the print *in situ*.

"Why wasn't it here five days ago when we found the body?" the sheriff asked.

"It was here, " District Attorney Rossman explained, repeating what the coroner's physician had said to him, "only you didn't see it because it was invisible. An impression made in freshly spilled blood is not discernible until after the blood has congealed."

Winney continued to deny his involvement in the murder of Catherine Srycock, even to a reporter from the Jackson Citizen Press who was granted an interview in Winney's cell and who flatly accused him of the murder. He insisted he was in Jackson throughout the evening of Thursday 26th February, but his alibi could not be supported.

It was his admission to the Finch and Bower burglary and the stealing of the .32 revolvers, plus that astonishing footprint, that weighed heavily against him and he was committed to trial in May 1914 in Jackson County Court.

The chief evidence against him was the print of his iron shoe in the pool of blood beside the victim's body, and the medical testimony which made it clear to the jury why that print was not seen when the body was discovered and why it became visible several days later when the blood had dried. Against such learned testimony, the bewildered accused could only say that he had not killed Mrs.Srycock, that he was never in her kitchen on that day, and that someone must have stolen or made a copy of his iron shoe and made the print with it.

In court, proceedings were drawn out because of the need to write down everything for Winney. He sat next to his defence attorney, Mr. Kirkby, and his clerk, and read everything that was being written down by the clerk

When he first took the stand, the court adopted the innovative method of writing all the questions on a blackboard so that Winney could read them and answer verbally.

Winney was first questioned about his upbringing. He stated that his mother had died in 1905 when he was aged 11, and that although his father was still alive, he had been brought up by his grandmother who lived in Spring Arbor, not far incidentally from the Srycock farm.

He stated that he had left his grandmother's place in early February 1914, and went to Jackson where he took up residence in the Adams block of the Y.M.C.A. Prior to that, he had visited the Srycock farm on at least four different occasions. On one occasion, he had stolen a ten-dollar note from the old woman.

When he first came to Jackson, he had sold his horse to a man called Clayton Brown for $65. He had received $25 in cash, and the balance consisted of two promissory notes totalling $40 which he had not yet received.

Winney confirmed that the arrest for the murder was not his first such arrest. About two years earlier, whilst in Detroit, he had stolen a shirt and 30 cents. On that occasion, he had been arrested and had served "as many days in the Detroit house of correction as I got in cents".

Asked to detail his movements on the night of 26th February, Winney replied that he had been with a girlfriend up to about 5 p.m. when he left her to go to the Y.M.C.A. building, that he had met two other girls he knew outside the Johnson funeral home on Mechanic street and had stood talking to them for a few minutes. He named them as Teresa Brown and Josephine Preston. He had

then gone to his room at the Y.M.C.A. where he had rested and read for a bit.
He left the Y.M.C.A. sometime between 7.45 p.m. and 8.15 p.m. and had gone to the Paris restaurant, and from there to Miller's Pool Room on South Mechanic Street, where he had remained until approximately 11 p.m. He identified two men he had been with at the pool room as Clare Roberts and Earl Herrington. At around 11 p.m., he had left the pool room and returned to the Adams block where he had gone to bed.
"Did you steal a horse and cutter rig from Jackson and Main street that night?" asked Attorney Kirkby.
"No sir, I did not."
"Did you know of one being taken?"
"No, sir."
"Did you ride anywhere in any sort of conveyance that night?"
"No, I did not."
"Were you out of the city of Jackson that night?"
"No, I wasn't."
"Did you shoot and kill Mrs.Srycock that night, or at any other time?"
"No, I did not."
"Have you any knowledge as to who murdered her?"
"No sir, I haven't."
"Were you in the company of any young man that week?"
"Yes sir, a young man named Everett Eng of Detroit. He used to be a bellhop at the Otsego."
Winney was unable to remember whether he saw Eng on the day of the Finch and Bower hardware store robbery. He stated that he had burglarised the store on his own.
"When you burglarised the store, did you have in mind that you would steal the guns and go out and murder Mrs.Srycock?" asked Attorney Kirkby.

"No, I didn't."
"Why did you steal the guns?"
"I am sure I don't know."
"Was it because you were hard up and needed the money?"
"Yes, that was the principle reason."
"If this was so, why didn't you take any other disposable property?"
"There was no other property there which appealed to me to be so easy to dispose of."
Winney stated that he had only between forty and sixty cents on him at the time of his arrest, and he was unable to cash the promissory notes he held for the balance of the sale of his horse.
"What did you do with the $25?"
"I have been having the devil of a good time."
"In what way did you have a good time?"
"By treating the fellows and being a good fellow, just the same as any fellows have a good time."
"Were you away from your room again after 11 p.m. that Thursday night?"
"I had an awful headache and I got up and dressed and went downtown to get some headache tablets but the drugstores were closed and I did not get any."
"How long were you away from your room that time?"
"I should say not more than fifteen minutes."
"What time did you get up to go downtown?"
"I don't know. I should think I had been in bed for at least an hour or an hour and quarter before I got up."
"What time did you get up on Friday morning?"
"I don't know but I generally don't get up until ten o'clock."
Winney stated that on Friday morning he had gone to the Jackson Cushion Spring Company to apply for work, and that he had expected to start work the following Monday.

"When did you fire the revolver, before or after you went to the factory?"
"After I went to the factory."
"What did you do with the gun?"
"I took it to my room and placed it in the bureau drawer."
Winney had denied witness reports that he had been heard to be washing some clothes in his room. He said he had not washed, or attempted to wash, any clothes on that day and did not think he had remained longed than usual in his room after returning from the factory.
Winney confirmed in response to District Attorney Rossman that he had told Sheriff Strobel he would find some guns in the bureau drawer of his room at the Adams, along with some ammunition. He could not say how one of the guns, a calibre .32 model, had turned up in the cell block where he was being held, and insisted he was being set up.
Employees from the Paris restaurant could not recall Winney having been there on the night of the murder, and no-one at the Y.M.C.A. remembered seeing him that night, although one witnessed testified that he had seen someone like Winney talking to two girls on Mechanic Street at around 5 p.m., and another witness testified he had seen Winney around 5.30 p.m. going towards the Y.M.C.A.
Winney was challenged about some "written" conversations he had with Leo Costlow, the train robber whilst they were in the same cell. In particular, he was questioned about the comment in one note which stated "notches on his gun butt." Winney denied that he had written any notes to Costlow but had written to himself. He had been requested to do so to write out his alibi, and the reference to "notches" implied that it was not the first time he had been arrested.

Winney denied that he had confessed to the Finch and Bower robbery because it was a lesser offence than the murder of Catherine Srycock. He admitted he had lied to officers when first questioned in connection with the robbery, but denied he had quickly changed his mind when it became apparent that his interests would be better served by a burglary conviction than for the murder conviction the sheriff's department were trying to pin upon him.

Despite his denials, it did not take the jury long after a four-day trial to find Harold Winney guilty of first-degree murder. The evidence of the bloody footprint was simply too overwhelming. This alone was the pivot upon which the murder conviction succeeded against Harold Winney despite other obvious lack of evidence against him, or even evidence that supported his claim to be in Jackson on the night of the murder.

Harold Winney was lucky to escape the ultimate death penalty, and was sentenced to life imprisonment by the judge.

Still protesting his innocence, Harold Winney made two appeals to the State Supreme Court. Both appeals failed to change the verdict.

During the long years of imprisonment that followed, Winney's thoughts kept returning to that mysterious footprint in the blood.

Since that footprint was the chief piece of evidence in the prosecution case which proved him guilty, all other evidence being disprovable or circumstantial, he reasoned that it must also contain the chief proof of his innocence, and he had to find a way to show that.

But how could he show that the evidence of the bloody footprint was flawed? Simply to argue this fact in a court of law was useless. His lawyers told him that all legal arguments had been exhausted. Numerous pleas to the parole commissioners had also failed.

What was clear to Winney himself was that someone had taken his iron shoe, or a copy of that iron shoe, and pressed it into the victim's blood to make him out to be a murderer. It was an argument he had always maintained since his arrest.

If that had been done before his arrest, then he was lost. There was no way he could prove his innocence because the State's argument was this was what had happened anyway, and that it had happened during the commission of the murder itself.

However, if he could prove somehow that the bloody footprint that convicted him could not possibly have been made until after he was in jail under arrest, and that someone had entered the sealed off Srycock farmhouse to make the print whilst he was in jail in order to make the State's case against him more convincing, then the State's case would collapse like a pack of cards.

He could accept the conviction and prison sentence for the burglary of the Finch and Bower hardware store, but that was a minor misdemeanour compared to first-degree murder.

As the months and years dragged by, it became more and more plain to Harold Winney that if he was going to get any help at all, this help would have to come from scientific sources. Winney discussed this many times with his lawyer without success.

One day, Winney heard through prison grapevine of the work of a micro-biologist named Pieter Keyzer who had been successful in disproving (or proving) evidence in a number of cases linked with blood and prevailed upon his lawyer to contact Dr. Keyzer.

Dr. Keyzer was intrigued enough by Harold Winney's arguments to want to try an experiment to determine whether an error had been committed at the trial in the inference drawn from that fatal footprint.

He set up a series of experiments on the rate of coagulation of blood in the Riverside Packing Company in Jackson in 1932. By then, Harold Winney had been in prison for 18 years, consistently fighting to prove his innocence.

Dr.Keyzer chose to use the blood of pigs because of their similarity to human blood. His tests showed that an impression made in blood as soon as 30 seconds after the blood has been spilled will be visible immediately. Although the edges of such an impression were slightly distorted, the impression itself was not obliterated and remained clearly in the blood.

An impression made much later after the blood had been spilled, and had partly coagulated or dried, retained a clear outline sharply edged. Dr. Keyzer found that the sharpness of the impression depended upon the extent to which the blood had coagulated.

From these experiments, Dr. Keyzer came to the unshakeable conclusion that the deputies who had investigated the murder of Catherine Srycock would have seen that footprint in the blood immediately upon their first arrival on the scene if it had already been there, and therefore made by the murderer. The footprint could not possibly have been there five days later if it was not already there on the first day of the investigation by the police.

Armed with this knowledge, he made careful preparations for a crucial demonstration before the relevant prison and sheriff's authorities, as well as the district attorney's office and Winney's defence attorney.

He chose a winter's day the following February when the temperature and atmospheric conditions were almost identical to 26th February 1914, the day of the murder.

From the same kitchen floor where the body had been found, Dr. Keyzer sawed pieces of board which were fashioned into several large trays. He then had an iron shoe constructed identical to the one Winney had worn on that day 19 years before.

The scene of the final test was in a room in the state penitentiary at Jackson, and the assembled participants included the parole commissioner, prison officials, State police, and several members of the jury which had convicted Harold Winney. Winney himself was also present.

Outside the room were some deputy sheriffs waiting to be called. These deputy sheriffs had been those who had seen the original bloody footprint.

Dr. Keyzer produced his four trays, which contained samples of pigs' blood. He explained that the trays contained blood spilled from pigs which had been killed 24, 48, 60 and 101 hours ago.

He now spilled blood from a freshly killed pig into another tray, and asked Winney to step into it with his iron shoe.

To the amazement of the intent onlookers, the impression made by Winney was immediately visible in the fresh blood, and remained so.

Dr. Keyzer now asked Winney to step into the other trays containing blood, leaving a print of his iron shoe in each tray. It was immediately seen that the impressions made in these trays varied in sharpness of outline according to the degree of dryness of the blood.

The scientist now called in the deputies who had found the footprint of Winney's iron shoe in the blood of the murdered woman five days after the murder had taken place.

"I want each of you," Dr. Keyzer said to the deputies, "to pick out the print which most resembles the one which you discovered at the Srycock farm."

Each deputy unhesitatingly pointed to the print made in the blood that had been spilled 101 hours previously.

"So you see, gentlemen," the scientist said to the gathered assembly, "if the murderer of Mrs.Srycock had left his footprint in her blood, the deputies would have seen it when they were first called to the murder scene, not five days later. And since that footprint was made at least four days after the shooting of the old woman, Harold Winney could not possibly have made it because he was in the sheriff's jail and had been there for two days."

Thus science triumphed where the law had failed!

A parole meeting was hurriedly convened by the prison authorities, attended by Winney's attorney and the district attorney's officers, and after months of legal argument, it was announced that Harold Winney's life sentence had been commuted to 25 to 50 years, and he was to be given immediate and indefinite parole with conditions.

The announcement by the parole board was given to Winney in his cell by Warden Peter F.Gray on 13th March 1934, almost 20 years after Winney's original trial. Winney's face must have been a joy to behold.

One condition of the parole was that he should not return to Michigan until the expiration of his maximum sentence, i.e. until May 1964 if he lived that long.

Harold Winney went to live in Toledo, Ohio where he married, had two children and got a job in mechanical engineering, a trade which he had learned in prison.

He would never, of course, recover the 20 years he had lost languishing in prison as an innocent man, or get over the pain and stigma of being branded a murderer.

It was also too late for anyone to answer the questions that were exposed from the moment Dr. Keyzer proved Harold Winney to be innocent of the murder of Catherine Srycock.

Who did actually kill the old woman?

Was it someone who could not wait for the old lady to die, and gain access to her 40-acre homestead and to her money?

Someone perhaps who was bitter at the way the Jackson County Court rejected an application for guardianship of Mrs. Srycock's financial affairs?

We will never know.

The other vital question that remained unanswered was :

Who planted Harold Winney's iron shoe, or a copy of it, in her blood?

We will never know that either, but if there was ever a brilliant "frame" that was almost foolproof, this was it. It took 20 years to expose the "frame".

4.   1951 : Birmingham, England

HANGED, BUT WAS HE INNOCENT

Monday 22nd January 1951 was a cold, wet day in the large Midlands city of Birmingham, England and it was lunchtime when the telephone rang in Edward Road police station.
The call was taken by one of the few female detective inspectors in England at that time, Detective Inspector Helen Beattie.
"Can I help you?" she asked.
The caller was a woman who refused to give her name. She said she was worried about the strange circumstances at a house at number 6 Back Clifton Road, Balsall Heath where there had just been a pregnancy. However, no-one had recently seen the expectant mother, and there were rumours of a death of an infant.
She added that no doctor or nurse had been seen going to the house.
DI Beattie was concerned enough to send out two uniformed sergeants to make discreet enquiries around Clifton Road, which was a typical Victorian-style residential street lined with back-to-back terraced houses.
In such neighbourhoods, residents lived so close to each other that almost everyone knew everyone else's business and the two sergeants found that the pregnancy at number 79 was no secret.
Reporting back to their headquarters, the two sergeants said that the house was occupied by a deaf man named William Watkins and his wife, Florence. The couple already had a three year-old child named Peter. They reported that neighbours had confirmed the expectant birth, and that Watkins had told these neighbours his wife

had delivered a baby on Saturday night in the presence of the local doctor and midwife. None of the neighbours had, however, been invited into the house to see the new-born infant, and there were rumours that the mother had in fact miscarried.

DI Beattie decided that the matter needed to be looked into further, and drove to Clifton Road accompanied by another policewoman, WPC Christine Coutts, and a male colleague, Detective Sergeant James Black.

After repeated hammering on the front door, it was eventually opened by a tall, unshaven man with greying hair.

"Eh?" he asked, cupping his hand to his ear.

DI Beattie repeated that they were police officers, and asked if he was Mr. Watkins.

"Yes. What do you want?"

"We would like to see your wife," the inspector said slowly.

"Well, she is upstairs in bed, ill like," the man told them.

"She had a baby on Saturday night."

"Oh, can we come in then and see the baby?"

"Well, I was sort of washing it over like and something happened," the man said, a bit distractedly.

Detective Sergeant Black repeated the police request to see his wife, and the man stepped aside to let them enter the shabby house, shutting the door on the gathering of inquisitive neighbours outside. It was not every day that a police car visited Clifton Road!

Once inside, the officers were led up the stairs to the front bedroom where a woman lay in bed looking very pale and ill. It seemed to the officers that she was in need of medical attention.

"Where is the baby?" DS Black asked Watkins.

Without a word, the man led them out of the room to a back bedroom whose door was securely fastened by copper wire.

After unfastening the copper wire, the man pushed open the door and gestured DS Black to enter. He found himself in a room which was full of old clothes and general junk. A metal wash-tub stood in the middle of the cluttered floor, with a pile of old and dirty clothes heaped on top of it.

Watkins removed the pile of dirty, old clothes and then the lid on which the clothes had been piled. DS Black found himself looking into a tub half-full of water in which lay a pillow-case. The lower half of an infant's body was sticking out of the open end of the pillow-case, and the top half which covered the head was immersed in the water.

Watkins was weeping as he lifted the corpse out of the tub. "It's quite all right, officer," he said, "I'm not frightened of it now."

DS Black found that the body stuffed head-first into the pillow-case was that of a new-born baby boy with curly hair.

"Who cut the umbilical cord?" DS Black asked.

"I did, with a pair of scissors," Watkins replied.

Black went back next door to report to Inspector Beattie what he had found. The senior officer decided to send out WPC Coutts for more C.I.D. back-up, and took Watkins downstairs.

Despite the cold January day, the house was unheated and the fire had not been laid. DI Beattie asked Watkins to see to the lighting of the fire, and to boil a kettle for some cups of tea. Watkins however seemed very slow-witted and both tasks were beyond him, and the police themselves ended up lighting the fire and brewing the tea.

Questioning Watkins proved to be a difficult task. Either he misunderstood the question because of his deafness, or he was genuinely too slow-witted to provide proper answers.

They gathered, however, that neither Mr. or Mrs. Watkins had made any arrangements for the birth of the baby. He kept repeating that the child had slipped from his fingers into the water whilst he was washing it and his wife had shouted for him. He had panicked when he found the baby was dead, and had not known what to do. He had buried the afterbirth in the garden.

The police officers also learned that he and 'Mrs. Watkins' were not legally married. Upon the arrival of Detective Chief Inspector Oliver Quinton and Detective Inspector James Mitchell from the local C.I.D. in response to DI Beattie's request for back-up, it was decided that as 'Mrs.Watkins' was not the legal wife of the man, she could testify against him under current English law and proceeded upstairs to take her statement. Watkins accompanied them up the stairs.

To spare the woman's feelings, she was addressed as 'Mrs.Watkins' by the officers during her questioning. She confirmed in her statement to the officers that she had given birth to a baby boy in the early hours of Sunday morning, and that no arrangements had been made at all for either a doctor or midwife to be present, or for the arrival of the baby. She stated that they already had one child and had not wanted another.

Watkins clearly could not follow what was going on, and after she had made her statement, he asked her what she had said.

"It's all right," she told him, "I've told them the same as you have."

Police then called an ambulance to take 'Mrs.Watkins' to hospital for medical attention, and made arrangements to have three year-old Peter taken into care, before asking William Watkins to accompany them to Edward Road police headquarters where he was questioned further.

Asked why the child was in a pillow-case, he replied :"I was washing it over the top of the pillow-slip like." Some of his answers to questions asked could be described as unintentionally ambiguous. It was as if he had not understood the purport of the questions. One such answer was "I couldn't have done" in response to a question that asked if he had lifted the baby out of the water after it had fallen in.

He was then charged with the murder of the infant, and appeared before magistrates the following morning dressed in the same clothes as he had worn the previous day, shabbily dressed without collar or tie. He was granted legal aid, and remanded in custody for eight days. It was his 49th birthday.

William Arthur Watkins was born of simple parents in Birmingham, and although his deafness was never diagnosed as a child, he had probably been deaf since birth because he always appeared slow-witted. He appeared to have had sufficient hearing to get by, and attended normal state schools instead of going to one of the two specialist schools for the deaf in Birmingham, the Royal Institution for Deaf & Dumb Children at Edgbaston or the day school for the partially hearing at Gem Street. As a consequence, he never learnt sign language and never mixed with any other deaf people.

As a young man, Watkins was interested in politics and for a time, was even the chauffeur to the Conservative parliamentary candidate during the 1939 by-election campaign in one of the Birmingham seats.

By trade, he was an enameller at the local Raleigh bicycle factory where he had been employed for some years, including the war years. It was probably during his call-up for the Second World War that led to his diagnosis of deafness, for he was rejected as being unfit for service.

He married his legal wife, whom he called Doss, before the war and fathered four children by her before walking out on them in 1946 and taking up residence with a young girl named Florence May White, who took to calling herself 'Mrs. Watkins' whilst they were living together.

There was an age gap of at least 25 years between Watkins and Florrie White, and although he treated her well and was a good father to their son Peter, the 'marriage' was under some strain at the time Florrie was expecting her second child and it was apparent that Watkins' common law wife did not want the baby. She refused to go to the pre-natal clinic, and made no preparations for the new baby. There were money problems as well, notwithstanding the steady wages coming into the house earned by Watkins.

There were those in the neighbourhood who thought that Florrie 'Watkins' had as much to answer for the death of the infant as Watkins himself, perhaps more, not because of her neglect of her circumstances and lack of interest in the pregnancy but also because of the lies that she told neighbours about the preparations for the birth.

This then was the background to the circumstances which led to William Watkins being charged with murder appearing for the second time before magistrates. On this occasion, medical evidence was presented by the pathologist who had carried out the post mortem on the dead infant. Home Office Pathologist Professor J.M.Webster stated that the child had been born healthy, although a month premature, and had died from asphyxia due to drowning. There were no marks on the child except for a small one on its nose.

The prosecuting solicitor, Mr. E.M.Pugh, told the court that Watkins told his wife, "I've done it. The baby is dead."

Watkins was also reported to have told the police that the baby had slipped out of his hands and dropped into the water. "If I drowned the baby, I did it in a panic," Watkins was alleged to have said.

The magistrates found there was a case to answer and committed William Watkins to stand trial at the next assizes.

This took place at Birmingham on 12th March 1951 before Mr. Justice Finnemore. The Crown prosecutor was Mr. R.T.Paget, KC, and Watkins was represented by a Mr. Fearnlet-Whittingstall, KC.

Watkins, as in his committal hearing, was scruffily dressed in a rumpled suit and wearing a shirt without a collar or tie. He looked stooped, gaunt and about 20 years older than his actual age.

It was clear from the beginning how difficult the trial was going to be for Watkins. It was evident that he could not hear what was being said, some of his answers causing muffled laughter in the court.

At one stage, Mr. Justice Finnemore was not amused by the laughter, and said that if it happened again, he would clear the public galleries.

Watkins could not understand, for example, the indictment being read out to him and being asked how he would plead. Eventually, a prison warder was brought up to the dock to stand beside him, and repeat the charge against him.

Watkins could speak, however. His answer of "Not Guilty!" was heard by everyone.

In his opening speech for the Crown, Mr. Paget told the jury that he would seek to prove that what they were about to hear was as clear a case of deliberate and premeditated murder as any they would ever find.

He alleged that 'Mrs. Watkins' and the accused had made no attempt to prepare for the arrival of the expected baby. No baby clothes were prepared and no medical advice was sought.

He would show the jury that neighbours in Clifton Road had observed 'Mrs. Watkins' growing pregnancy, and that the time was coming for the child to be born. "They enquired whether arrangements had been made, and in the presence of Mr. Watkins, she had told them she had booked Dr. Salmon and that a midwife was coming. That was quite untrue. Neither Dr. Salmon nor a midwife had ever been informed."

The prosecutor said that the mother's contractions began in the afternoon of Saturday 20th January, and she assured a neighbour that Dr. Salmon had been booked. Later that day, as the contractions became more frequent, Watkins told the neighbour he was going to fetch Dr. Salmon.

However, when the mother gave birth to the infant boy at 3.30 a.m. on Sunday morning, only Watkins was present in the room.

Pointing at Watkins, the prosecutor said that :"The accused then picked up the baby and pushed it head downwards into a pillow-case. In that state, head downwards in the pillow-case, he put the baby into a galvanised tub of water, and there the baby drowned and died."

Mr. Paget alleged that the next morning, Watkins had told a neighbour his wife had had a miscarriage, that he had fetched a doctor and midwife who were both now gone and would not be returning.

"All that was, of course, quite untrue. It was never intended that this child should live and that is why no arrangements were made for its birth, or its life. Arrangements were only pretended to have been made."

The prosecuting counsel said there could not be any possibility of a simple accident happening when a body of a child is put head-first into a pillow-case, then put into a tub of water, and pointed out that the childbirth and the killing had been concealed from neighbours.

The Crown's first witness was Florence May White who told the court that she had been living with William Watkins for five years. He had treated her very well, but when she learnt she was expecting her second child, she was upset. "The way things were between us, we did not want any more children."

She said that she had never even seen the infant, as Watkins had delivered it, and taken it away immediately afterwards as she was feeling too ill.

"Did Watkins tell you anything afterwards?" she was asked by Mr. Justice Finnemore.

"He just said he had dropped it in the bath." (This has of course a different meaning from her earlier statement to the police that Watkins had said 'I've done it. The baby is dead.')

Cross-examined by Mr. Fearnley-Whittingstall, Florence White agreed that she had been pressurised on several occasions by Watkins to go to the pre-natal clinic, but had not done so.

She agreed that at the time of her contractions, Watkins had wanted to go and fetch her doctor, but she would not let him.

She agreed that shortly after the birth, she had shouted out to Watkins to come to her and clean up the mess on the bed.

When William Watkins was called to the witness stand, he told the court that while he was being interviewed at the police station, a detective had slapped his face, saying that he was not going to stop there all night. He claimed the officer had said, "You know the girl has done it, and she is trying to blame you for it."

But when Watkins was confronted by the three officers who had questioned him, he said that none of them was the one who slapped him and Detective Chief Inspector Quinton was recalled to the witness box to confirm that none of the officers involved in the interrogation had used violence. He also denied that any reference was made to the possibility of charges being laid against Florence White for her part in the death of the infant.

"It seems inconceivable," Mr. Fearnley-Whittingstall commented, "that this man [Watkins] would have invented this story if it had not been true."

Put back in the witness box, Watkins confirmed that when he knew his wife was pregnant, he had urged her to go to the pre-natal clinic.

"My wife told me she did not want another baby, but I did not mind if we had another baby. Two or three times, I asked her to go to the doctor or the welfare but she did not go."

Watkins appeared to be confused about a number of questions. Every time he was asked one, he would look at the prison warder to have it repeated to him.

In his original statement to the police, Watkins had stated that he had gone downstairs and filled a zinc bowl of water that was still warm from the kettle, and added some cold to it, and brought the bowl upstairs. He had pulled a pillow-case off one of the pillows on the bed, and had wiped some blood off the baby with a shirt. He was holding the baby when his wife had shouted and he had slipped the baby into the pillow-case and dropped it into the water before going to his wife and cleaning the bed up. When he had gone back to the baby, he had found it was dead and panicked, not knowing what to do.

In the witness box, Watkins was grilled over his version of the events leading to the baby's death.

"I went to wash the baby. My wife was crying about the mess on the bed, and I turned round sharp and dropped the baby in the bowl in the water."

"Where was the pillow-slip then?"

"In the back bedroom. It had been put there for washing."

"What did you do after you dropped the baby?"

"I took all the bedclothes and put some clean clothes on the bed."

"Why did you not pick the baby out of the water?"

Watkins, obviously misunderstanding, replied "No. I left him in there. Well, I was worrying about the other child being awake and my wife crying."

"That bowl was half-full of water?"

"Yes."

"Was the baby head-first in or sitting in?"

"Head-first when I got it out."

"Did you see it go in?"

"No. It slipped out of my hand when I turned round sharp."

"Did you try to kill it?"

"No."

"How long were you tidying up?"

"I think about quarter of an hour."

"What happened when you came back?"

"Well, I saw the baby's head in the water and I carried it into the back bedroom, and I went to get this pillow-slip to put it in, but I could not and it dropped in the water and I left it there."
"Why could you not?"
"Well, my nerves."
"Did you put it inside the pillow-slip?"
"Yes. I went and put it inside."
"And put it back in the water?"
"Yes."
"When you carried the baby in, you put the lid on top and some clothes on top of that?"
"Yes."
"Did you put the baby in the pillow-slip when it was alive?"
"No."
"What did you do to the door?"
"I fastened the door with some string or wire to keep the other child from going in there."
The prosecuting counsel asked Watkins why his account now differed from the statement he gave to the police. Watkins replied that he had not known what he was saying part of the time because he was confused. They had had him in the police station so long that he could not remember.
The prosecutor then asked him :"Do you agree that if somebody put a live baby head-first into a pillow-case and then put that pillow-case and the baby into a bath of water head-first, they could do it with no intention save to kill it."
Mr. Fearnley-Whittingstall objected, "That is hardly a question this witness can answer. I would have thought it was an astonishing question. It is hardly a question which a deaf labourer below average intelligence can answer."
However, the judge interrupted :"It is obvious, is it not? If anybody puts a child like that into a bath of water you

would think it was for no other purpose but to destroy its life."

Then turning to Watkins, the judge asked, "Why did you lie to your neighbour about your wife having a miscarriage? Why did you tell her that unless it was because you had killed the child?"

Watkins could only say: "I don't know."

In his closing speech, Mr. Paget was extremely brutal.

"All the evidence indicates that this baby was not expected to live. Although it was one month early, no preparations for a baby that is expected to live had been made."

Referring to the events of the birth, Mr. Paget said: "He says that this baby slipped into the water because he was washing it and because his wife was crying about the mess on the bed. When it slipped into the water, he did not look to see whether it was head-first or otherwise, and he did not think of picking it out. Members of the jury, is that even a remotely credible story?

"It is said he panicked and lost his nerve. But did he? He had nerve enough to put that bath into the back bedroom, to cover it up with clothes, to wire-up the door, to take the afterbirth into the garden and bury it, to go and see a neighbour and tell her his wife had a miscarriage and also, untruthfully, tell her that the doctor and midwife had been there. Does this sound very panicky?"

For the defence, Mr. Fearnley-Whittingstall told the jury they had seen for themselves that both Watkins and his common-law wife were of comparatively low mentality.

"The prosecution say that this murder was planned. A planned murder? With this woman going round amongst her neighbours with her growing pregnancy for everyone to see?

"I have said Mr. Watkins is not in a particularly intelligent class of society and not particularly intelligent. But does one really imagine he could be so stupid if it was planned that this child would be destroyed when it was born? Because then there would be all the gossip from neighbours asking 'Where is the baby?', 'What has happened to it?' In the end, it would have been bound to have come to the notice of the authorities, as it has done."
The defence counsel went on, "This is a man of good character and there is no evidence that the other child, Peter, has not been affectionately looked after. He has been a good father. Does the evidence indicate that this man is a kind of monster? Are you surprised that he was a bit unnerved? It is a fairly unnerving thing for somebody who has no medical knowledge, no nursing experience, to see a woman in the process of childbirth or to see a woman immediately after the birth of a child."
Mr. Fearnley-Whittingstall said that Watkins' answer to one of the police questions "I could not have done" was one of the most significant points in the case, because it was the answer of an innocent man. A liar and a planned murderer would have answered differently.
In his summing up, Mr. Justice Finnemore told the jury it was clear that Watkins had been anxious to hide the birth of the infant.
"If this man was washing the baby and it fell into the bath, how could it have got head-first into the pillow-case? If he put the baby into the pillow-case before it went into the water, it must throw very grave doubt on to his story that he was washing the child properly at the time of the accident, as he has stated in court."
The judge said that the jury might feel that in the very least Watkins had acted with gross negligence and even callousness if he had taken no steps to rescue the baby

after it had fallen into the water. In that case, Watkins should be guilty of manslaughter at least.

"After all, nothing could be easier than to pick the child out. It would only take one second, two seconds, possibly three. He did not do it. As he said himself, he did not bother."

The jury retired at 11.50 a.m. on March 16th to consider their verdict, and were back in court by 2.15 p.m.

They found Watkins guilty of murder and Mr. Justice Finnemore donned the dreaded black cap, and sentenced Watkins to death.

Even then, there was a scene of tragic comedy in the court when Watkins turned to the prison warder by his side and asked, as he had asked many times throughout the trial, "What did he say?"

The prison warder looked at the judge, received a nod, and said to Watkins, "He says you are to be hanged."

II

At the very least, it had been a farce of a trial.

It has to be remembered that one of the principles of English law at the time was that an accused had to understand what went on during his trial. Clearly, William Watkins did not.

Indeed, if William Watkins possessed any knowledge of British Sign Language, and used that as a means of communication, it is probable that the outcome of the case would have been very different.

Although the jury had made no recommendation to mercy, it was widely believed that Watkins would not hang. Even the prosecuting solicitor at the committal hearing, Mr. Pugh, never thought that the case would end with Watkins being sentenced to death.

His plight attracted considerable sympathy, and a petition for a reprieve was set up. It stated that Watkins had made no effort to conceal the death from the police, that he was of low mentality with no previous convictions. Many felt there was reasonable doubt about his guilt of murder, and that at the very least, it was a case of manslaughter. The petition stated he had been handicapped at his trial by his inability to hear much of the evidence, that it was not satisfactory for information to have been relayed to him by a prison warder.

Watkins himself did not seem to realise how bad his situation was, for in a letter to Florence White, he wrote:

"Dear Florrie,
I was glad to see you and Peter. I am glad you are looking better. Dont worry about me I am O.K. we get plenty to eat and books to read and exercise outside every day. I hope Mum and Pop are alright remember me to them when you write. When you go up home dont forget yours and Peters identity cards and birth certificates, they are in that box in the cupboard and doctors cards. *I hope I shall soon be out and back at work.....*(author's italics)

One must question whether the defence counsel could have done better during the trial. Most certainly, Mr. Fearnley-Whittingstall was not deaf-aware enough to work out several opportunities to the advantage of his client.

For example, his cross-examination of Florence May White when she was in the witness box was an extremely poor piece of cross-examination. The witness should have been pressed to answer (a) why she had not gone to the pre-natal clinic when told to do so by Watkins, (b) why she had not let Watkins fetch the doctor - was this because Watkins did not in fact know she had made no arrangements?

The closing speech should also have been perfect for the rebuttal of the prosecution's remarks that she had told neighbours in the presence of Watkins that she had booked Dr. Salmon and a midwife - how could anyone be sure that Watkins had actually understood what she was saying to the neighbours? One only had to look across at the dock and see the prison warder helping Watkins to follow the trial; the jury had laughed hadn't they, along with those in the public galleries, on the occasions when Watkins completely misunderstood the questions being put to him, and gave answers way off the mark?

Defence counsel could also have said that Watkins' misunderstanding of questions being put to him in court, witnessed by everyone, cast grave doubt on the accuracy of the statements he was supposed to have given the police. How could the jury be sure that Watkins had misconstrued the police questions, and given incorrect answers, or statements that he thought answered the questions correctly?

It was also clear that the way Watkins presented himself in court, i.e. scruffily dressed, his low mentality, his hearing-impairment, may have contributed to an overall picture as an undesirable member of society, and influenced Mr. Justice Finnemore's rather biased summing up.

Whatever the failings of the defence, the petition for William Watkin's reprieve was rejected by the Home Secretary who gave a statement that he saw no grounds to interfere with the course of justice, and the famous executioner, Albert Pierrepoint was appointed to oversee the execution of Watkins.

In his last days, Watkins was visited in his condemned cell by his lawful wife and children, who forgave him for walking out on them in 1946.

III

William Watkins was hanged at Winson Green prison, Birmingham on the morning of 3rd April 1951.
Among the crowd outside the prison gates when the execution notice was posted were a number of his former workmates from the Raleigh bicycle factory.

5.   1959 : Perth, Australia

A BLEMISH ON JUSTICE

When the body of a 22-year old leading society girl was found murdered early on Sunday morning 20th December 1959, no-one would have known or guessed that it set the scene for one of the most tragic, bitter and enduring controversies in Australian legal history. A controversy which not only cast a blight on the integrity of the Australian justice system, but also cast a dark shadow on the honesty of the principal police officer involved, and on the professional integrity of sign language interpreters.

The morning began, as it had most Sunday mornings in the Perth, Western Australia suburb of Cottlesloe for engaged couple Andrew Dinnie and Jillian Brewer, with an appointment to play a round of golf on a nearby course.

Both keen golfers, with Miss Brewer almost frantically so (she had a large mural of Gary Player, the South African golfer, and expensive golf equipment in her flat), they had got into the habit of playing a regular round on Sunday mornings.

It was 8.45 a.m. when 30-year old Andrew Dinnie drew up in his car outside the modern, well-furnished ground floor flat belonging to Jillian Brewer to pick her up and take her to the course with him.

When she had not emerged through her front door after a few minutes, he switched off the engine, got out of his car and went up to knock on the door. There was no answer, and his attention was drawn to the bedroom window where his fiancee's French poodle named Christian Dior was jumping up and down barking wildly.

Concerned, he went back to his car, took his keys out of the injection, and after finding Jillian Brewer's flat key, let himself into the flat, one in a block of six at Stirling Highway, Cottlesloe.

There seemed to be nothing amiss, but in the bedroom, he found Jillian Brewer in bed. She looked to be asleep, with her left arm over a pillow which lay across her chest, and the sheet drawn up to her chin and folded over the pillow. It was only when he drew nearer that he realised there was a pool of blood about her head.

Jillian Brewer's mother lived in the next door flat, and Dinnie ran round immediately and informed her of the tragedy. He asked her to get the police and the doctor.

A squad of detectives from Perth Criminal Investigation Bureau led by Detective Sergeant George O. Leitch were quickly on the scene, securing it with tape and searching for clues.

The crime scene was also extensively photographed by police photographers.

About an hour later, at 10.30 a.m., the police pathologist Dr. Alva Thomas Pearson arrived and examined the crime scene.

The murder victim had been stabbed several times in the head and the body, and had also been beaten about the head. There were deep multiple wounds above the hairline, but the wounds on the body were not so severe. There was no sign of any struggle in the flat, and Jillian Brewer appeared to have been attacked as she lay asleep.

The stab wounds appeared to have been caused by a sharp instrument, but the head had been beaten about with a different, more blunt, weapon of which there was no sign in the flat. The skull appeared to have been fractured, and this was confirmed later at the post mortem which also showed that the most probable cause of death had been a wound in the neck which had severed the windpipe.

There were no outward signs of any sexual interference as a sanitary tampon was still in place, and nothing appeared to have been stolen from the flat, nor was there any apparent sign how the murderer had entered the flat, although there was an open window covered by a flywire screen. The back door was locked on the inside. Near the bottom of this door, there was a small rectangular flap which could be pushed open from the outside to allow small articles such as milk bottles to be left on the floor inside the door. The flap would then fall back into position under its own weight. The importance of this was not to be realised for four years.

Police were stymied by a seeming lack of motive, and clues. There were no fingerprints in the flat and no clue whatsoever as to the identity of the person who had killed Jillian Brewer. Detective Sergeant Leitch sent other squad members including fellow Detective Sergeants Balcombe and Patterson, and Detective Zanetti out to question neighbours and search for clues. The Head of Perth C.I.B., Detective Inspector C. Lamb, made a brief visit to the scene, but left the investigation in charge of Sergeant Leitch.

One factor which mystified the police investigators greatly was the silence of the French poodle, Christian Dior. The dog was the only one in the block of flats, and was notorious amongst the neighbourhood for its loud barking, and Andrew Dinnie himself stated that the dog was wont to bark furiously at anyone who came to the door, including him as well, but questioning of neighbours found no-one who could recall any noise during the night, much less any barking by the dog.

It had been a hot summer's night, and many flats had their windows open in an attempt to catch whatever breeze there was, and any prolonged barking or serious disturbance would have been heard.

A Mrs. E. McInerney, who lived immediately above the dead girl's flat, told police she had returned home just before midnight, and had seen Dinnie's car outside, and had heard and seen him drive off a few minutes later, but had heard nothing further during the night.

Police investigators questioning friends and neighbours of Jillian Brewer had her described as a happy, fun-loving attractive girl, slim with dark-hair, the grand-daughter of Sir MacPherson Robertson, the founder of a well-known Australian sweet-making firm, and a heiress in her own right.

Educated at a Melbourne secondary school, she had subsequently taken a course in interior designing and worked in this field for a leading Melbourne architect before taking a chaperoned finishing trip round the world, after which she had relocated to Perth, Western Australia about 18 months before her death.

She was not in any permanent employment in Perth due to her substantial means, but helped friends with dress-making, at which she was an expert, and the odd-spot of interior designing. She was in fact in the stage of making up her own wedding dress for her forthcoming marriage to Andrew Dinnie whom she had known for five months. They were due to get married in February. She had expensive tastes, enjoyed golf, and had a clean, well-kept and expensively furnished flat.

Police toyed with the theory that she had been the victim of a burglar who had observed her wealth, but the fact nothing was stolen from the flat put paid to that theory.

Her mother, who had followed her out to Perth and lived in the same block of flats, worked in a prestigious Perth shop, and had collapsed with the shock of her daughter's murder and was admitted to hospital.

On the Monday following the murder, Detective Sergeant Leitch told a press conference that public response to police appeals had been good, with several calls to the incident room which could help in their inquiry.

"No matter how insignificant the information may seem, we would like to hear it," Leitch told reporters.

He confirmed that police were linking the Brewer murder with the murder of another wealthy woman in January 1959, eleven months before.

On that occasion, Mrs. Patricia Vinico Berkman (usually called Pnina for short), aged 33, the mother of a nine-year old son, had been found by her lover, local radio personality Fotis Hountas, murdered in her South Perth flat, and the case was still unsolved. There were several points of similarity in the two cases:

- Both women had been stabbed repeatedly in the head and on the body.
- Both had come to Perth from the Eastern states of Australia.
- They lived alone in tastefully furnished flats. (Mrs Berkman's son did not live with her.)
- Both were killed late at night, and their bodies not discovered until the next morning, and with a remarkable coincidence, by their respective boyfriends.
- Both women were murdered in bed with no apparent signs of a struggle or disturbance, and no sign of any doors or windows being forced.
- In both cases, the murder weapons were not found.

However, Detective Inspector Lamb, Head of Perth C.I.B. at the same conference, refuted any links between the Brewer case and the attack on 17-year old nurse Alix Doncon at her flat nearby, also on Stirling Highway. She suffered from a fractured skull. This case was, said Lamb, separate and done by a different person.

There was a flurry of new excitement on Tuesday when it was announced that police had found what they believed to be the murder weapon. Detective Patterson, searching an area between a six-foot wooden fence dividing the block of flats where the murder victim lived from sheds belonging to houses in the next road, found a 2lb. lath hammer - a kind of hatchet - nestling against the foot of the fence.

The hammer was identified by the householder in Renown Street who stated it had been used to trim his lawn and hedges, and had been missed from its usual place on Sunday.

Forensic tests positively identified the lath hammer as the murder weapon, and a reconstruction of the crime scene suggested that the murderer stole the weapon from the garage where it was kept, vaulted over the fence to the block of flats, and thrown back over the fence after the murder had been committed.

A pair of dressmaking scissors with 8-inch blades found in a tray of dressmaking material in the victim's flat also reacted positively to chemical tests to detect blood, and fitted the description of the "sharp instrument" used to inflict the stab wounds about the head and body.

Despite these discoveries, however, the murder investigation entered its fourth day no further forward to finding the person or persons who did the crime, and as Christmas approached, C.I.B. Chief Lamb issued a warning to householders in the metropolitan district of

Perth : "Lock your doors at night. If you see a prowler or notice any suspicious person, move quietly to a telephone and tell the police."

Inspector Lamb said that the police had received about 130 calls from members of the public about the murder, and some reports had proved valuable.

"From the information we have acquired during the past few days, we are gradually building up a picture of the events up to and immediately after Miss Brewer's murder," said Inspector Lamb. "We are also building up a mental picture of the type of killer we are looking for."

He said that many car movements had been reported to the C.I.B, and all had been checked and accounted for. He also said that two facts had emerged from the intense investigation led by Detective Sergeant Leitch.

> Two people had said they heard a dog bark briefly in the vicinity of the flat between midnight and 1 a.m. - this could have been the murder victim's poodle, Christian Dior.
>
> Several months ago, Miss Brewer had temporarily mislaid her flat keys, and had forced the latch of the living room flyscreen to enter. This latch had not been mended. However, detectives were still not able to explain a hole near the latch of the bedroom screen.

Lamb confirmed that police were not discounting the theory they were searching for a multiple killer who could also be responsible for the South Perth murder of Pnina Berkman, but discounted any links with the attack on Alix Doncon nearby on 8th August. Both the South Perth and Cottlesloe murders did not conform to the pattern of the attack on Miss Doncon, said Lamb.

As Christmas and the New Year passed, however, no further developments were made in the investigation, and the murder was gradually dropped from the front pages of the newspapers, and the investigation wound down. However, the police made it routine whenever they arrested anyone for loitering, prowling, burglary or other sexual charges, they would routinely question the offender to determine if he was responsible for the murder thus several men were questioned over the next few months, but no charges were brought on the murder.

Interest in the case was reactivated when police announced on 16th June 1961 that they had arrested a man for the murder of Jillian Brewer. No mention was made of any link with the murder of Pnina Berkman.

They gave the name of the arrested man as Darryl Raymond Beamish, aged 20, of Garden Street, Swanbourne, Perth.

II

At this stage, it is necessary to look at some minor criminal activities taking place during the Australian summer of 1960 and 1961.

A series of petty burglaries and break-ins, together with faces at windows, prowlers and loiterers, plagued Perth, as were the more worrying reports of little girls being sexually interfered with in parks.

On 7th April 1961, Alan John Elliott, aged 20, a panel beater, appeared before Magistrate T. Ansell at Perth Police Court accused of several counts of burglary, and stealing the sum of four Australian pounds. He was sentenced to four months imprisonment. He was told through a sign language interpreter by the magistrate : "We need to lock up people like you as long as possible."

On the same day, Darryl Raymond Beamish, then aged 19, a labourer, came up twice before the same court and the same magistrate, on four charges of sexually assaulting young girls which were admitted. He was remanded in custody until the afternoon session for sentencing. On his second appearance later that afternoon, the magistrate sentenced him to seven months gaol (this being the term used in Australia for imprisonment).

He was told through his sign language interpreter by the magistrate that he was a pervert, and deserved greater punishment.

On 4 August 1961, John Snell, aged 21, appeared before Perth Police Court and Magistrate Ansell who gave him the maximum possible sentence for the charge of "loitering and looking into windows at night". Magistrate Ansell commented to the accused through his sign language interpreter : "If there was a bigger sentence possible, I would impose it. The public needs to be kept safe from people like you."

Deaf people, then, were being treated excessively severely by the police court in Perth for even very minor offences.

Behind the scenes - that is, in the police cells and elsewhere - there was something shameful going on, particularly with Darryl Raymond Beamish who was being subjected to an ordeal that was to ultimately see him charged with murder, a crime for which he was considered by many people after he had been sentenced to be innocent.

III

Darryl Beamish was born on 12th April 1941 to George William and Frances Merle Beamish of Swanbourne, Perth. He was the youngest of five children. His brother was already aged 19 and away serving in the Australian armed forces when Darryl was born, and there was a gap of ten years between the youngest of his three sisters and himself when he was born so he was very much the baby of his family, with minimal or little contact bonding with his siblings as he grew up.

The fact that Beamish was born Deaf distanced him further from his siblings, the more so since he went to the West Australian School for the Deaf at Mosman Park as a boarder from the age of 5 years, coming home usually only for the odd weekend and at holiday periods.

At school, where he remained until he was aged 16 leaving with no qualifications, Beamish was not academically bright. As John Orr Love, former Principal at the West Australian School for Deaf and Dumb Children for 28 years until his retirement in 1955, at which time Beamish was aged 14, was to testify in evidence at the trial, Beamish was a slow learner with a language capacity in reading and writing below that of a seven year old child. That did not mean, Mr. Orr Love hastened to add, that Beamish was below average intelligence, only that Beamish could not read or write well. He could communicate his thoughts and understand well enough in his own sign language.

The trial of Darryl Beamish opened at Perth Criminal Court on Monday 7th August 1961 before the Chief Justice, Sir Albert Wolff, and a jury of nine men and three women.

The Crown were represented by Chief Prosecutor R.D.Wilson, whilst Beamish was represented by a court-appointed junior defence counsel, Athol C. Gibson.

Beamish pleaded through his sign language interpreter not guilty to the murder of Jillian MacPherson Brewer on the night of 19-20 December 1959.

Addressing the jury, Prosecutor Wilson said the facts to be presented in court would fall into two phases, One would deal with the killing of the girl in her Cottlesloe flat in the early morning of 20 December 1959.

The other phase would relate to the period from April to June of that year (1961) when Beamish was either in police custody or in prison and being questioned by the police.

"The Crown," said Wilson, "alleges that Miss Brewer died from multiple injuries, some of which were inflicted by a hatchet stolen from a garden and others by a pair of scissors which the victim used for dressmaking."

A total of 14 witnesses would be called by the Crown, and the first witness, Andrew Dinnie, an accountant-secretary, of Torrens Avenue, Cottlesloe related the events of the night of 19th December and the morning of 20th December 1959. He stated that he and Miss Brewer were to have married on 11th February 1960. He had been introduced to Jillian Brewer in August 1959, and from the time they started going out together, he did not know of any other male person with whom she associated.

He said that he and Miss Brewer had played cards and rearranged the bookcase at her ground floor flat in Brookwood Flats, Stirling Highway on their return from an evening out earlier, and he had left at almost exactly midnight. Miss Brewer was then sitting up in bed nude. It was a hot night, and the poodle Christian Dior was asleep under the bed.

Asked about the dog, he stated that it was highly strung and had a loud piercing bark. He would expect it to bark at the noise of any intruder in Miss Brewer's flat.

He related how he had returned the next morning at 8.45 a.m. for their game of golf, and had to let himself into the flat because there had been no answer. The dog was jumping up and down excitedly inside the front bedroom window. He went into the bedroom and saw Miss Brewer lying on the bed with a sheet pulled up to her chin and her face covered with blood. She appeared to be dead.

Cross-examined by Athol Gibson, Dinnie confirmed that they had had sexual intercourse around 11.30 p.m. before he left just before midnight. He denied that he had any argument with Miss Brewer on that night. They used to have squabbles, but had never had any serious argument.

The police pathologist, Dr.Pearson, was the next witness, and he used a life-size dummy to point out to the jury the location of the numerous wounds on the victim's body. He confirmed his opinion that death had been due to the wound which had severed the windpipe.

Cross examined, the witness stated he believed death had occurred between 2.a.m. and 6 a.m. and that the wounds allegedly made by the pair of scissors were made some time after the injuries allegedly made by the hatchet.

He confirmed that there was no evidence the girl had struggled whilst being wounded.

Allan Farquharson Drummond, chief technologist of the Public Health Laboratory Service testified that he had examined several articles. The head of the hatchet gave a positive chemical reaction when tested for blood, and group A human blood was found on the inside of the blades of the dressmaking scissors. This blood group matched Jillian Brewer's.

The next two witnesses gave evidence of the finding of the hatchet, but the next witness was potentially damaging to the defence, and was subjected to intense questioning by Athol Gibson.

Raymond Wallace Toms, an unemployed labourer, said that on April 8th 1961, while he was in police custody, he saw Beamish write on the bitumen floor of the exercise yard at Perth Central Police Station the words : 'Cottlesloe where drunk I kill lady 7 months.' The writing appeared to have been done with a piece of plaster or some mortar-like material.

Cross examined by Athol Gibson, Toms testified he thought Beamish had written the words after lunch. The writing was still visible in parts the next day. He could not remember whether anyone was with Beamish before or at the time the writing was being done.

Gibson : "Did you notice the words 'Not me' alongside this writing?"

Toms : "No."

Gibson : "And there was nothing to prevent persons in this yard from walking to and fro across the writing on the bitumen, was there?"

Toms : "No, nothing."

Re-examined by Mr.A.J.Dodd, assistant prosecuting counsel, Toms said that to the best of his knowledge, there were no detectives or other police officers in the yard before or at the time Beamish wrote the words. The only people in the yard had been three or four other prisoners beside himself and Beamish.

Detective Sergeant Kevin McKay testified that at about 4.30 p.m. on April 8th, he had examined the printed words on the floor of the yard.

Cross examined, DS McKay stated : "I knew Beamish had been questioned by detectives concerning Miss Brewer's death, and I notified DS Leitch of the writing on the floor."

- No, he had not taken any steps to have prisoners removed from the yard so that the writing could not be obliterated.

- No, he had not taken steps to preserve the writing.

- No, he did not have any photographs taken of the it.

- No, he did not see the words 'Not me' on the floor.

The last of the nine witnesses for the prosecution who testified that day was on the stand longer than most, in fact for most of the afternoon, and for most of it, under cross examination by Athol Gibson.

This was Florence Mary Myatt, described in court as a public relations officer for the West Australian Deaf and Dumb Society.

She testified that she had been present on April 7th and April 8th at Perth Central Police Station with Detective Sergeant Leitch and Detective Deering when they had interviewed Darryl Beamish. She testified that she had acted as interpreter throughout his questioning, and was satisfied that Beamish had understood the questions.

She was again present at Fremantle Gaol on 12th June when Detective Sergeants Leitch and Balcombe had questioned Beamish, although this time she was not interpreter. That time, the role was fulfilled by the Reverend Chetwynd, and she affirmed that Beamish appeared to understand what the Rev. Chetwynd was saying to him.

In cross examination, Mrs.Myatt said that for someone like Beamish, she had to alter the ordinary phraseology of English. She had explained to Sergeant Leitch that she had to put questions to Beamish in simple language.

Asked by Mr.Gibson how she had interpreted the words : 'I want to warn you that you are not obliged to say anything unless you wish to do so', she said she had forgotten what she had said. She might have said :'If you do, it may be against you or bad for you.'

She knew that Beamish had a limited English vocabulary.

The interview with Beamish began at 10.15 a.m. after his appearance in Perth Police Court, and she was with Beamish until about 3.30 p.m. that day. Describing the day's events, she said that Beamish was taken to

Brookwood Flats by Leitch and Deering at about 11 a.m., and then back to the C.I.B. office in Perth where he was questioned further.

At about 2.15 p.m., Beamish was taken back to the police court where he received a sentence of seven months' imprisonment on four charges of aggravated assault

Gibson : "Did you know that this was the first time he had ever been sentenced to imprisonment?"

Myatt : "Yes."

Gibson : "And immediately after receiving that sentence, he was taken by the police officers back to Brookwood Flats?"

Myatt : "Yes."

The judge, Sir Alfred Wolff, interrupted at this stage with a question asking if Beamish had been questioned in the car going to Brookwood Flats.

Myatt : No, not in the morning. Neither going or coming back."

Continuing the cross examination, Mrs.Myatt told Gibson they had got back to Brookwood Flats at about 2.30 p.m. When Beamish was asked whether he had ever been to Brookwood Flats, he stated he had been there to see a girl named Ann.

When the car was parked outside a dentist's where she was due to have an appointment, Leitch had asked Beamish if he had hurt the lady and that they wanted the truth. She had interpreted to Beamish : 'We want truth. My boss wants truth. Will you tell us the truth because we have clever staff', and she had pointed to the police station.

Beamish had dropped his head to his hands and said, 'Yes, I did hit or hurt lady.' He was crying.

She confirmed that on the morning of 8th April, she was present when Beamish was again interviewed. Leitch

Harold Winney, after his release from prison. (Chapter 3.)

Winney's distinctive shoe, which helped to convict him. (Chapter 3.)

William Watkins. (Chapter 4.)

Crowds waiting to read the execution notice at Winson Green prison, Birmingham, on the morning of Watkins' hanging. (Chapter 4.)

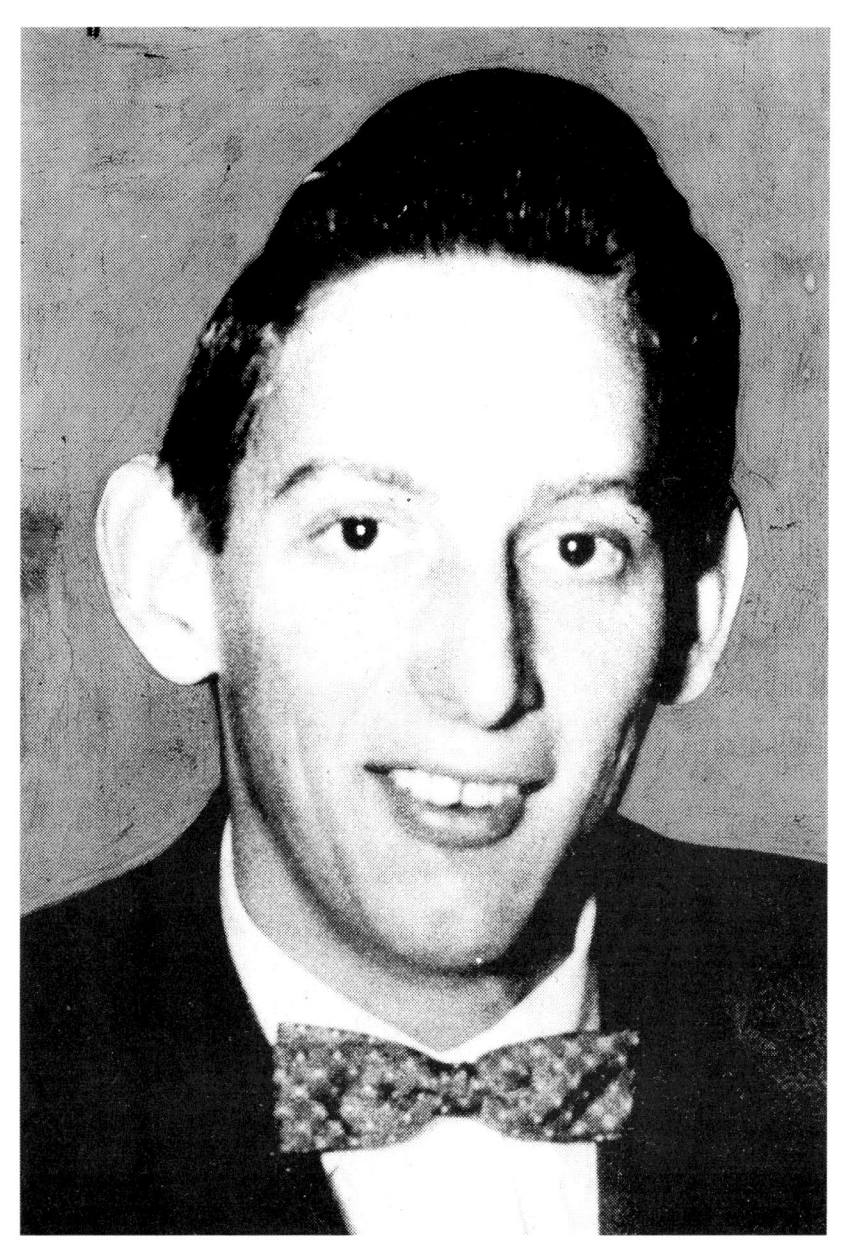

Darryl Beamish. (Chapter 5.)

Jillian Brewer relaxing in her flat, a few weeks before her murder. (Chapter 5.)

Detective Inspector Lamb, Perth C.I.B. chief, examining the weapon that killed Jillian Brewer. (Chapter 5.)

Eric Edgar Cooke. (Chapter 5.)

wrote down the questions, and Beamish wrote down the answers.

In response to Athol Gibson's question, Mrs.Myatt confirmed that when first questioned by Leitch, Beamish had vehemently denied killing the lady.

She confirmed that in October 1960, she had interpreted for the police when Beamish pleaded guilty to a number of minor stealing offences.

Under re-examination by Prosecutor Wilson, Mrs.Myatt testified that Beamish appeared mush happier once he had said : 'Yes, I want to tell the truth.' Beamish was never confused by any questions.

Only two witnesses for the prosecution testified on the second day of the trial, and for all but the final ten minutes of that day, it was the examination, cross-examination and re-examination of Detective Sergeant George Leitch that took up the time in court.

Leitch stated that at about 11 a.m. on 7th April, he and Detective Deering had questioned Beamish at Brookwood Flats in the presence of Mrs. Florence Myatt who acted as interpreter.

Beamish had initially said that he knew nothing about the murder of any woman at the flats, but after they had returned to the city and were parked outside a dentist's in Hay Street, he had said to Beamish : 'I want to find out the truth. You know we have lots of things to help us, like scientific aids and photographs. My boss wants me to find out the truth. Did you hurt the lady?'

At this stage, defence counsel Athol Gibson made an objection, and at the request of the judge the jury retired while counsel addressed him.

Mr.Gibson said that his objection was on the grounds that the statements had been obtained by questionable means without any proper warning or legal advice and were not admissible as evidence.

Sir Albert Wolff said that he should have objected to Mrs.Myatt's testimony the previous day, and ruled the evidence was admissible.

Continuing on the return of the jury, Leitch told Chief Crown Prosecutor Wilson that Beamish indicated he wanted to tell the truth, that he had hit the lady with an axe when she was asleep on a bed. Beamish had indicated with his hands the axe was as long as a tomahawk or a hatchet.

At the C.I.B office, Beamish said that when he first saw Jillian Brewer, she was standing up and had no clothes on. (Although it was not alluded to at the trial, in the Appeal this statement was taken as proof that Beamish was in fact there because though there was no proof that Jillian Brewer had left her bed after the departure of Andrew Dinnie, she must have done so, perhaps to wash or douche herself because there was no pathological evidence at the post mortem of any sexual intercourse which Dinnie said they had had, and Brewer was wearing a sanitary towel when she was found the next morning). Beamish had been on the outside looking through a window, and had stated he got into the flat through a back door. When asked why he had killed the lady, Beamish had said : 'Head mixed up.'

Leitch said that Beamish had told him he stabbed Jillian Brewer three times in the stomach with a pair of scissors that were in the bedroom, but could not remember whether he had stabbed her anywhere else. Beamish stated at first he had got the axe off a wood heap, but later pointed to the floor of a garage in Renown Street and admitted he had got the axe from there. Beamish said he had gone to the garage looking for money, and that he had not told anyone else he had killed Brewer.

Leitch said he had again interviewed Beamish on 8th April in the presence of Deering and Mrs. Myatt who interpreted. Beamish wrote down answers to questions which he (Leitch) had written down, and had signed the document.

Leitch stated he next saw Beamish on Monday 10th April at the Central police station, and had asked Beamish if he had written the words on the bitumen floor. Beamish had nodded his head, and had written on a piece of paper, 'Not me kill lady Cottlesloe.'

Leitch wrote back,'Why have you changed your mind?', and Beamish had written in response,'Father he said say nothing.' When he had asked Beamish why he had written what he had said on the bitumen floor, Beamish had shrugged and he had not pursued the conversation.

Most of the printed words had been rubbed off when he went back to photograph it, and in the photographs, only the words Cottlesloe and where were still identifiable.

Leitch testified that on the afternoon of June 12th, he had gone to Fremantle Gaol with Sergeant Balcombe, the Reverend Chetwynd and Mrs.Myatt to re-interview Beamish. Dr.Ernest J.T.Thompson, psychiatrist for the insane at Fremantle Gaol was also present. He pointed out the document containing the written questions and answers that had been given on April 8th, in which Beamish had said he had killed the lady. He had said to Beamish, 'You told me that you went out the back door. Is that right?' Beamish had replied 'Yes', and he had asked 'Could it have been the front door?' Beamish had shrugged and said it could have been.

Beamish had been asked if he had been to the flat before, and he had said yes. Beamish had then said his father had told him, 'Athol Gibson say, "Say nothing."' and they had not pursued the questioning.

Leitch said that when questioned again on 16th June, again with the Reverend Chetwynd and in the presence of Detective Sergeant Balcombe, Beamish had said he did not want to say anything. He was then charged with the murder of Jillian Brewer.

In response to questioning by prosecuting counsel Wilson, Leitch said that it was about nine-tenths of a mile between Beamish's home and Brookwood Flats where Jillian Brewer lived, and that the words '7 months' would have been meaningful to Beamish, given that he had only the day before been sentenced to that term of imprisonment for aggravated assault.

Leitch underwent a severe grilling during his cross examination by Athol Gibson.

- Yes, he had looked at the dog when he first came to Brookwood Flats on 20th December. It was a quick look and he had not seen anything wrong with it.

- No, nobody in Brookwood Flats had heard the dog bark that night.

- Yes, only two people thought they had heard Miss Brewer's dog bark about the time of the crime.

- Yes, it could have been some other dog, not Miss Brewer's.

- Yes, he had questioned a big number of suspects about Miss Brewer's death.

- Yes, he may have had some scientific aids which could prove or disprove Beamish had committed the offence.

- Yes, he had photographs which might have satisfied him Beamish had not committed it.

Leitch proved to be an adroit witness, rarely if ever giving Gibson an opportunity to turn the advantage in favour of his client. He flatly denied that he had frightened Beamish into making an admission.

Gibson : "Beamish will say that before the admission you were poking him in the chest and shaking your fist in his face. What have you got to say to that?"

Leitch : "I would say Beamish is definitely wrong."

Gibson : "Would it be true to say Beamish was crying?"

Leitch : "Not before he made the admission, no."

Gibson "At the first interview at the C.I.B. when you asked him where he hit the lady and he took a piece of scrap paper and made a drawing, did he not draw two beds?"

Leitch : "No, he did not."

Gibson : "And did you not say, No, one bed?"

Leitch : "No, I did not."

Gibson : "If there was nothing to hide, why did you destroy that sketch?"

Leitch : "I did not think it was important."

Gibson : "Not important? But it was evidence. Beamish says he didn't kill Miss Brewer."

Leitch : "He had admitted on many occasions that he had hit the lady on the head."

Gibson : "And he drew that too, didn't he? Where is that sketch now?"

Leitch : "It was a pretty rough sketch. It was destroyed the next day after I had interviewed Beamish at length. The wound marks were shown on the top of the head."

Gibson : "Beamish also wrote down the words, 'Not me kill lady Cottlesloe', did he not?"

Leitch : "Yes."

Gibson : "Where is that paper now?"

Leitch : "I destroyed it."

Gibson : "When you saw Beamish on April 10 you had serious doubts whether to accept his confession, didn't you?"

Leitch : "I was giving it consideration. With others I formulated a plan on April 1o which was put into execution and worked."

Gibson : "And what new evidence did you get between April 10 and June 12?"

Leitch : "None, I had decided to let the matter go for some considerable time, so that Beamish could make up his mind."

Gibson : "You did not charge Beamish on getting this confession but let the matter go for two months?"

Leitch : "Yes."

Leitch said that the night before Beamish was charged with the murder, he went to see his parents to explain things to them.

Re-examined briefly by Prosecutor Wilson, Leitch said that Detective Deering and Mrs.Myatt were present throughout his interviews with Beamish on April 7th and 8th, and were in a position to see his conduct towards Beamish.

When he came off the witness stand, Leitch had been giving evidence for over five hours, and the final ten minutes of the day were given to the Reverend Christopher Chetwynd, who said on oath he was Church of England minister and chaplain to the Mission for Seamen in Fremantle. He confirmed that he interpreted at the interviews with Beamish on 12th and 16th June, and was quite sure that Beamish understood all the questions put to him by Detective Sergeant Leitch.

IV

The court was packed for the third day of the trial, for it was on this day that the defence was to begin its submission, and it was expected to put the accused on the stand.

The first hour and half of the morning were taken up with the remaining Crown witnesses, including the recall and re-examination of the police pathologist Dr. Pearson for clarification over the possible differences in the time of the death of Miss Brewer. Dr. Pearson stuck to his opinion that death had occurred between 2 a.m. and 6 a.m., though he did agree that it was possible that the period between the infliction of the wound to the neck which severed the windpipe and the time of the actual death could have been as long as two hours - in other words, it was possible that the neck injury could have been caused at midnight, the time Andrew Dinnie said he left the flat.

Then the moment everyone was waiting for arrived. Athol Gibson called his client to take the stand.

Darryl Beamish was to be on the witness stand for the rest of that day, and for the whole of the next day.

Opening for the defence, Gibson said that Beamish would deny absolutely that he had anything to do with the murder.

"Beamish will tell you that the admissions, such as they are, were obtained by the police under threats and intimidation. And further, that many of the answers which he gave and which have been given in evidence were given as a result of suggestions put to him, either by Mrs.Myatt, an interpreter, or by the police officers concerned."

"It will be shown that this particular crime had a great deal of publicity. There was an inquest at which a great deal of the evidence you have heard here was given. Details of that evidence were published in the Press so that very much of the matter contained in the alleged confession was common knowledge to Beamish and members of the public."

Gibson first took Beamish through details of his childhood and education to put him at ease, eliciting from Beamish that he was the only one in his family who had ever been in trouble with the police.

Beamish said that on Friday 7th April, he was in Perth Police Court in the morning, and was taken to the top of Central police station by persons he now knew as Detective Sergeant Leitch and Detective Deering. Mrs.Myatt, an interpreter whom he knew as Flo, asked him about a murder. He had said, 'Murder what? Don't know.'

He was then taken in a car with Leitch, Deering, Flo and another policeman who was driving. The car stopped at some flats in Cottlesloe that he knew as Brookwood Flats.

He had said to Flo :"What for?" (*Note* - this may have been how it was translated, but in Auslan as well as British Sign Language, it is more likely to have been <u>signed</u> as 'Here what for?' - see section VI).

Flo replied, "Murder", and he had said, "I don't know."

Beamish had asked what murder, and Flo had said "Lady". Flo told him he had to tell the truth.

Gibson : "Did you commit this murder?"

Beamish : "No."

Beamish said that Leitch had said 'Murder' and pointed at Beamish's chest.

Gibson : "Do you know that a murder is a killing?"

Beamish : "No."

Beamish stated that Flo had been aggressive, telling him not to tell lies and kept pushing him. She had told him that the lady had been murdered on 20th December 1959. He had not heard of the murder before.

Leitch was shaking a fist in his face, and poking him in the chest, and made him cry.

Leitch had asked him if he had been looking through windows at the flats, and he had told Leitch he had not.

He had known a girl named Anne who lived in one of the flats at Brookwood Flats, and he had been to see Anne when she was living there (in 1960 and 1961) but had not been to the flats before Anne lived there.

They then drove back to Central Police Station in Perth, where Leitch showed him two photographs. One was of a man, a lady and a dog and the other was of a bed on which somebody was covered over. Flo talked about the murder, and had said 'You know.'

Beamish said he had replied he did not know, and Leitch teased him by poking him in the chest and pointing at him again.

Gibson : "Did you at any time tell Leitch that you had hit the lady with an axe?"

Beamish : "No."

It was the next day, Beamish said, that he wrote on a piece of paper. Flo told him, 'mixed up head' and he wrote 'Head'.

The questioning at the police station had to stop when he had to return to court and was sentenced to 7 months imprisonment on four charges, but immediately after the court appearance, he was taken back again to Brookwood Flats where Leitch knocked the key of a back door onto the floor with a piece of wood, and put a piece of wood through a square hole in the door and got the key.

Chief Justice Wolff interrupting (to woman interpreter in the court) : "Tell him Leitch said he did that."

Interpreter : "He says, No - Leitch."

Beamish said Leitch opened the door, and he followed Leitch into a bedroom.

Gibson : "Have you been in that bedroom before?"

Beamish : "No, never."

Leitch told him he had hit a lady on the head, and Beamish had said, 'No, no.' and sat on the bed and cried.

Leitch had asked if he had killed the lady, and Beamish had said he had not. Leitch talked about a dog, and Beamish said he had never seen any dog. When they got outside, he followed Leitch round the streets to a garage where Flo told him, 'Looking for money.' He did not know why she had said that, and Leitch asked if he had taken an axe from the garage. He had never taken such an axe from any garage.

Later, back at Central Police Station, Leitch had asked him to draw a lady and put marks on the drawing. He did such a drawing, and Leitch looked very pleased with it.

Beamish said the next day, 8th April, he was taken to the top of the Central police station again where Leitch wrote down some questions on a piece of paper, and Flo was there and told him to write down certain answers.

Gibson asked Beamish to look at the second question on a document which said, 'Yesterday you told us you killed the lady at night on 20 December 1959.', and asked Beamish : "Did you write down 'Yes'?"
Beamish : "Yes."
Gibson : "What made you write 'Yes'?"
Beamish : "Leitch."
Gibson : "Did you kill the lady?"
Beamish : "No."
Gibson : "Did you ever go to Miss Brewer's flat before?"
Beamish : "No, not that one."

Flo had told him to write down he had gone to the lady's bedroom and hit her with an axe and a pair of scissors. He wrote untrue answers to some questions because Leitch threatened him with his fist. He also wrote down answers because Flo had told him to. For example, to write down that he had a scooter in December 1959. He did not have a scooter then.

Gibson : "Did you get an axe from over the fences as you have written?"
Beamish : "No."
Continuing his evidence, Beamish stated that Leitch had taken him to Brookwood Flats three times on April 7th but did not take him to the flat again on Saturday, where he was in an office upstairs at Central Police Station with Leitch, Deering and Mrs.Myatt. They had not talked about Jillian Brewer or the murder, but Mrs.Myatt and himself had talked about several other matters.
When he left the C.I.B. office, he was taken to the lock-up at Perth where another boy had written on the floor : 'Cottlesloe drunk.' and asked Beamish what happened. Beamish, using soap, had written back on the floor : 'I kill lady not me. 7 months.'
Beamish stated that Leitch asked him questions on paper when no interpreter was present, and he had written on the paper 'Not me kill lady Cottlesloe.'
He was not told he did not have to answer any questions. This had been shown to him on a piece of paper.
Beamish testified that on June 12, he was visited in Fremantle Gaol by Leitch, another detective, Mrs.Myatt, the Reverend Chetwynd and a 'fat man' (prison psychiatrist Ernest Johnson) when Leitch showed him a piece of paper and said, "Murder" and pointed his finger at him. Beamish said he did not say anything, but after he had read the paper, he put his head down and cried a little and said to Leitch, 'Not murder'. He did not understand the Rev, Chetwynd's interpreting.
During Beamish's lengthy cross-examination by Prosecutor Wilson, Beamish repeated the allegations he had made when being examined by his defence counsel. He insisted that:
- Flo told him to write down 'I want to tell truth'.

- Leitch kept poking his finger in his chest, waving his fist in his face and making him cry.
- Flo had asked him to sign how big an axe was.
- When Leitch had asked why he had looked through a window at a lady, Flo had told him to say 'Sexy', but he had shaken his head and said, 'No, didn't.'
- He had told Leitch and Flo he had not killed the lady, and Flo had told him to write down 'Head mixed up.'
- Answers to a number of written questions were not true. None of the answers to questions to do with the lady at the flat were true. Flo had told him to write them.

He testified that Leitch had asked him if he had killed a lady at South Perth (Pnina Berkman), and Flo had told him to say 'Kill lady at Cottlesloe, not kill lady at South Perth.' He had cried, and they (Mrs.Myatt and Leitch) had said, 'Please, kill.' He had shaken his head and cried.

Beamish said he had been telling the court that Leitch had not been telling the truth in evidence, but admitted to a document showing his police record of 24 previous charges of stealing. He disputed that he had committed 24 offences. He admitted to the four charges of assault relating to four little girls aged between four and five whom he had taken to King's Park and sexually interfered with, masturbating while he inserted a finger inside their vaginas, for which he had received seven months imprisonment.

Prosecutor Wilson took Beamish through a cross-examination of the second visit to Brookwood Flats, when Beamish had earlier testified that it had been Leitch who had opened the back door by the means described (i.e., of knocking the key out of the keyhole).

Wilson : "Are you sure it was not you who opened the back door?"

Beamish : "No, Leitch."

Wilson : "Did you not say 'Had wire before'?"
Beamish : "No, didn't."
Leitch had told him to push the door, and he did it.
He had followed Leitch through to a bedroom, and no, he had never been in that room before, but Leitch had told him 'Different bed.' In the bedroom, both Flo and Leitch made him do some hits on the bed, and he had cried when he did that.
About the dog, Flo had told him to bark, so he had made a movement with his fingers to stimulate a dog barking, and he had copied Flo's sweeping gesture. He did not understand the implication of that sign.
Outside the flat, Leitch had asked him about an axe, and he had told Leitch he had thrown the axe next door, but it was because Leitch was already pointing in that direction. He had followed Leitch round to a garage, and Leitch had pointed to the garage. Flo told him he had gone there to look for money. He did not know why she had said that, but guessed that this was where the axe had come from and had said so.
He reaffirmed that the words he had written on the floor at Perth lock-up had been 'I kill lady not me.'
Beamish stated that on June 12th at Fremantle Gaol, he could not remember whether he was told by Mr.Chetwynd he might or might not speak, but after each question, Mr.Chetwynd asked 'Do you understand? Is it true?' Beamish stated the Reverend Chetwynd was wrong when he said that he (Beamish) had answered every question. Beamish said he cried at the interview because Leitch teased him by pointing at him, and a piece of paper. He did not cry because he had killed a lady, he had not killed a lady.
Wilson : "Between 12 and 16 June at Fremantle Gaol, was a man named Monty Beamish there?"

Beamish : "Yes, cousin."
Wilson : "Did you speak to him?"
Beamish : "Yes."
Wilson : "Did he tell you to deny your confession and say you had not killed a lady?"
Beamish : "No, didn't."
Throughout his testimony, Darryl Beamish either refuted allegations he had said or done something, insisted that Leitch and Mrs.Myatt were lying, insisted that all his written answers to questions put by Leitch were suggested by 'Flo', and stood by his assertion he had not killed Jillian Brewer, and when he stood down, he had spend over ten hours on the witness stand.

V

The fifth day of the trial saw several defence witnesses being called, including Beamish's parents who were hostile towards Detective Sergeant Leitch and Mrs. Florence Myatt.

George Beamish described Leitch as aggressive in his conduct towards them. Leitch's manner, he said, was such as to get his blood warmed up a little bit.

He described Mrs.Myatt as someone whom he felt was working for the police, and refuted suggestions from the Prosecuting Counsel Mr.Wilson that he had arranged a private meeting at her home. Beamish's father stated firmly that he had never arranged any private meeting at Mrs.Myatt's home. What private meeting there had been was held at the premises of the Deaf and Dumb Society, and was done at the request of a solicitor, not at his request.

He said that Leitch had been insistent on knowing the whereabouts of Alan Elliott on 4th April. Elliott had been at his home up to approximately, he thought 9.30 p.m., but his wife had said it was 10 p.m. He felt Leitch was trying to link his son to Elliott's burglary activities.

He confirmed that he had been told of the 24 charges made by police against his son, but did not believe that Darryl had committed that many offences. He felt the police had no proof that Darryl had committed these offences, and denied that he had been present when Alan Elliott described how Darryl had pushed out the key of a lock and got into premises in Hay Street, Perth.

He stated that on the night of 19th December, he and his wife had attended a Masonic lodge gathering at Nedlands and had returned home at between 12.15 and 12.30 a.m. and Darryl had come in a few minutes later, and went to bed after speaking to them. He had noticed no change in his son's behaviour then, or afterwards.

He stated that he had told Darryl several times between 10th April and 16th June not to talk to police, particularly Leitch, without his solicitor Athol Gibson being present, instructions which Leitch had ignored. He recalled that on 16th June, he saw Darryl at the C.I.B. office at about 11.45 a.m., and Darryl had said to him : "I didn't do it, Dad. I didn't do it. They have me all mixed up." He had immediately asked Athol Gibson to come over, and Gibson had told Darryl not to speak to anyone, not even Mrs.Myatt.

Asked by Prosecutor Wilson if he had said to Detective Sergeant Leitch, 'If you do charge him you will be sorry', the witness replied : "I don't think I said those exact words. I might have."

The father confirmed that his son had not told him about the occasions he had taken four little girls to King's Park.

Mrs.Frances Beamish, in giving evidence, confirmed that on the night of 4th April when detectives had visited her home looking for Alan Elliott, she had told them he had left at 10.30 p.m., but realised afterwards it was between 9.30 and 10 p.m. He had been watching television at their house.

Asked about the night of 15th June when detectives came to their house and Leitch asked her husband to sign a statement about the whereabouts of Darryl on the night of 19th December 1959, which her husband refused to sign, she was asked why not.

Frances Beamish : "I don't know actually. Because he was aggressive, most likely."

She confirmed that it had taken her and her husband a while to think back and remember what happened on the night of 19th December 1959, but once she had done that, she knew that Darryl had come home within 10 to 15 minutes after they had returned from Nedlands and had gone to bed soon after. She had not noticed anything unusual about her son's behaviour then, or since.

Mrs.Beamish said she was not friendly with Mrs.Myatt but there had not been any ill-feeling between them.

She confirmed that she had been with her husband when they visited Darryl at Central Police Station on April 12th when her husband had instructed Darryl not to say anything without the presence of Athol Gibson. She said that was not the first time Darryl had been told that instruction, and this instruction was communicated to Leitch. She said that Darryl had communicated to her and her husband that the police and Mrs.Myatt were mixing him up, making him say or agree to things he did not mean or understand.

Another witness, Elizabeth Penny, a dental nurse living at Brookwood Flats, recounted that on two occasions during February 1961 she had encountered Darryl Beamish on two consecutive evenings, and he had indicated by writing on a pad he was looking for a girl named Anne. On the first occasion, at her suggestion, Beamish had gone upstairs to look for her. On the following evening, she took Beamish to the flats next to Brookwood Flats and later saw him driving away in a car.

On neither occasion was there anything unsettling or objectionable about Beamish's behaviour.

Another witness for the defence confirmed that on the night of 19/20 December, she had seen a man on a vacant block looking at Brookwood Flats, and shortly after the dog had barked once or twice, she heard a man call out for a taxi which did not stop, and then somewhere in the distance, the sound of a scooter being driven off.

At the end of that day, the judge ordered the jury to be sequestered for the weekend. They were to remain in their hotel, but could go for walks or trips provided they were under escort. They could read, listen to the radio, play cards, watch television or discuss the case, but they were expressly forbidden to talk to members of the public.

On the Monday, a witness named Susanne Delaney testified that she had lived in Brookwood Flats for a period of time from November 1960 until March 1961, and had known Beamish for two or three years and was able to communicate with him in Auslan (Australian sign language).

Beamish used to call her Anne, and sometimes called in the greengrocery shop where she worked and talk to her. On one occasion, she had been in Beamish's Holden car, and testified that Beamish had been to her flat. Miss Delaney said that Beamish had always behaved properly with her, and had never even attempted to kiss her.

Consultant psychologist Jeffrey White, appearing for the defence, stated that he had examined Beamish in Fremantle Gaol between 28 July and 4th August, and prepared a report on the tests he had carried out on the defendant.

Ratings indicated that Beamish had at least average intelligence, but functioned as a mentally defective person when he was asked to communicate with other people. This deficiency arose from a serious lack of adequate educational background and a lack of training in methods of communication with other people.

Cross-examined by prosecuting assistant A.J.Dodd, White denied that he had told the gatekeeper at Fremantle Gaol on 28 July that he was a solicitor, and stated that he was not qualified in any profession other than psychologist. He felt that Beamish was more defective in his use of language than the average deaf person but had no basis of comparison because he did not know the average deaf person's vocabulary. In his opinion, however, he thought Beamish would know the meanings of the words 'lady', 'hurt', 'axe', 'door', 'dog', 'kill', 'blood', 'fence' and 'pillow'.

John Orr Love, the retired principal of the West Australian School for the Deaf and Dumb, although called as a defence witness, fell into a trap when being cross-examined by the prosecution, and unintentionally gave credence to the prosecution case when he was asked about Mrs.Florence Myatt.

Wilson : "What kind of character does Mrs.Myatt bear?"
Witness : "I know nothing about her character at all."
Chief Justice Wolff, interrupting, "Mr.Wilson wants to know in general terms what sort of character does she bear?"
Witness : "I think she bears an excellent character."

This observation was to be used with devastating effect in the Judge's summing up, and by the judges in the Court of Criminal Appeal later.

Athol Gibson tried to repair this damage in his closing address to the jury when he submitted that the only evidence against Beamish was an alleged confession or alleged confessions which were wrong in many particulars and obtained in peculiar and unreliable circumstances without the presence of defence counsel. There was, Gibson said, no direct evidence to connect Beamish to the crime at all

The prosecution's closing speech to the jury also referred to the alleged confessions. Mr.Wilson submitted that the confession must have been made by the killer of Jillian Brewer, and asked the jury to remember that Mrs.Myatt, a public relations and welfare officer for the Adult Deaf and Dumb Society, was present throughout. On later occasions, with the Reverend Chetwynd interpreting, Beamish confirmed the confession which was consistent with the general background of the crime.

Beamish, Wilson said, was a sexual pervert, a thief, and a liar. He lived less than a mile from Brookwood Flats, and was accustomed to prowling at night. The crime, Mr.Wilson argued, could only have been committed by a person having the characteristics and attributes of Beamish. He asked the jury not to allow sympathy for Beamish's disability to cloud their consideration of the question whether he was guilty or not guilty.

The Chief Justice also referred to the alleged confessions in his summing up to the jury, and referred to the interview at Fremantle Gaol with the Reverend Chetwynd interpreting. What sort of cleric would Mr.Chetwynd be, the judge asked, if he stood there and watched Detective Sergeant Leitch allegedly force Beamish into making a statement? Yet that was the indictment levelled against Mr.Chetwynd.

Mr.Chetwynd, the judge said, had said in no uncertain terms in his evidence that Beamish understood everything that was put to him, but Beamish in evidence said he had said nothing but cried. Mr.Chetwynd said he read to Beamish categorically everything in a written document and Beamish had nodded his head. Beamish did not say in the witness box that he did not know what he was saying at interviews with the detectives. What he did say was that he said certain things in response to allegedly cajoling by Mrs. Myatt to whom he referred as Flo.

"If all those things are true of Mrs.Myatt and Detective Sergeant Leitch, what a pair of unmitigated scoundrels they are," the judge said. "It has been put to you that they cooked up a story which the accused, in his weakness or his innocence, has subscribed to. It is not that he is saying to you,'I did not know what I said.' What he is saying to you is, 'I said what I did because of those things that were put to me by Leitch and by Flo.' If these charges against Leitch and Mrs.Myatt and everybody connected with them are true, they were vile charges."

The jury would have to judge whether the verbal and written statements made by Blemish were in fact confessions of something Beamish had really done. In his opinion, the verdict would rest on the circumstances relating to the obtaining of the confessions.

"The jury must consider whether the Crown has entirely made out its case that the confessions were got in the way which was adduced in the evidence and whether they can safely accept the confessions as acknowledgements of guilt."

The jury of nine men and three women only took an hour to bring in a verdict of Guilty.

Chief Justice Sir Albert Wolff donned the black cap, and passed the sentence of death upon Darryl Beamish. "You

have been found guilty of the wilful murder of Jillian MacPherson Brewer on 20th December 1959. There is only one sentence which I can pass, and that is you shall be at a date to be announced hanged from the neck until you are dead."
Beamish shook his head and wept as the verdict was communicated to him, and signed something.
"What was that?" Chief Justice Wolff asked the interpreter.
Interpreter : "He said, Not Guilty."

VI

With hindsight, it is easy to pick holes in the case, to criticise the performance and the mistakes of the defence counsel, Athol Gibson, during the trial. It has to be remembered, however, that he was only a junior counsel and possibly not experienced enough at this level.
It is difficult to unravel the transcript or transcripts of the alleged confessions, a point that was made by the three justices hearing the appeal but this does not excuse the fact there were too many inconsistencies in the evidence presented before court which were not properly or inadequately challenged.
Not enough either was made of the fact that there was no direct evidence to link Beamish with the murder of Jillian Brewer. Also, why for instance did the police concentrate on the Brewer murder, and scarcely bother with the other murder which they had always maintained was linked, the murder of Pnina Berkman?
The manner in which Gibson chose to question key witnesses, notably Leitch and Mrs.Myatt, was curious to say the least, for he failed to challenge key elements of the confessions, another point which was constantly

referred to in the Criminal Court of Appeal by the three justices who criticised Gibson for his failure to challenge the prosecution before they had gone too far with outlining the confessions in detail, and before Mrs.Myatt was called to the stand, and also for failing to challenge the decision by the Chief Justice over admissibility of the confessions. Gibson also failed to challenge Mrs. Myatt on Beamish's assertion that it had been principally her that had suggested the words Beamish had written down in the question and answer statement taken on 8th April at the Central police station. Beamish, for instance, had great difficulty in distinguishing between the words 'ask', told', 'said', and also had difficulty with questions containing the word 'why'. The following extract from the trial transcript during his cross examination by Prosecutor Wilson illustrates this:

Wilson, referring to the writing on the floor at the police lock-up yard in Perth : "Why did you start to write?"
Beamish : "Boy told me what happened."
Wilson : "Do you mean boy told you what happened, or boy asked you what happened?"
Beamish : "Boy said what happened."

The choice of witnesses for the defence was also curious to say the least. Where, for example, was the testimony of a DEAF witness for Beamish, or an expert on the linguistic characteristics of Auslan. There are a number of alleged sayings in the confessions which would never have been said by a heavy Auslan-user like Beamish - the grammar and structure of those sayings are all wrong. For instance, Beamish would never have said, as he was alleged to have said in response to a question by Leitch 'What time of the night was this?' - 'I haven't got a watch.' Those are Mrs.Myatt's words, not Beamish's who would have signed something entirely different. Similarly, not enough was made of the fourth alleged confession submitted by the prosecution, the writing on the floor of the prison lock-up. One can well believe Beamish when he insisted that he wrote 'I kill lady not me' because that is the way a user of Auslan would grammatically structure a sentence in writing, and was it not curious that no-one really bothered to preserve the evidence when it was first seen, instead of reconstructing two days after the writing was allegedly made what everyone *thought* it was? A more accurate description would be, what everyone except Beamish *thought they wanted to see* as having been written on the floor.

Why, for example, did the defence call upon a psychologist who had absolutely no knowledge of deafness, deaf culture and deaf issues? Was there not any qualified psychologist or psychiatrist who could give an insight into a person like Beamish?

And it was a defence witness who gave Mrs.Myatt such a glowing character reference that Chief Justice Wolff and three Appeal Court judges all remarked upon it and chose to disbelieve Beamish.

To be fair, perhaps, it was the 1950's and the 1960's - an era when deaf people, especially those who used sign language as their principal means of communication, were treated as second-class citizens, of no value, and who were expected to be kept in their place by teams of welfare workers and other Deaf and Dumb Society employees.

Any Deaf person who has lived during that era will be able to visualise the circumstances in which Beamish found himself, and the role played by a person like Mrs.Myatt. To call her an interpreter is an insult to present-day professional interpreters who have codes of ethics and training to function effectively in their role.

It will be remembered that already earlier that year, Alan Elliott and John Snell had been labelled 'people like you', as if they were part of an untouchable caste, by a magistrate in Perth Police Court and punished out of proportion to their misdemeanours. Furthermore, over in Sydney in eastern Australia, there was another Deaf person also being tried in court for murder.

For the time, therefore, treatment like Beamish received is not surprising. Deaf people were 'looked after' by people like Mrs.Myatt who were termed welfare workers. Many were also often clergymen. This breed of people were often loved by their charges, but all too often also had an unfortunate tendency to assume a role as God, Judge and Jury to any Deaf person who had committed a misdemeanour or who otherwise fell foul of the law. Such people very rarely 'interpreted' as such for their clients, especially where the police were involved. The only occasions when they truly 'interpreted' was in court or in church ceremonies. On any other occasion, many were wont to act independently of their clients. For example, at a job interview, the welfare officer would discuss the merits or demerits of employing the Deaf person with a prospective employer while the Deaf person just sat there like a dummy, at the end of which so-called interview, the Deaf person would be given the good news that s/he had a job and could start the following Monday.

And so it was with the police. The welfare worker would often discuss things with the police, and appear to act on his or her own initiative as an 'interrogator' on behalf of the police. She or he would push or prod the Deaf person, accuse the Deaf person of lying, and 'interpret' by one means or another information which she or he felt the police desired to know, often without the Deaf person being fully aware what she or he was saying. Sometimes, even, the police would not pursue the charges in the belief that the matter had been sorted out with the Deaf person! The author has witnessed this with other Deaf people. Any Deaf person living between 1950 and 1970 will say that these things happened frequently, either to them or to someone else.

This is not to say that Mrs.Myatt fell into this role, but to read between the lines, one has to assume that something like this went on with Beamish.

Let us take, for example, the alleged confession that happened in the car parked outside the dentist's in Hay Street, where it is not disputed either in the trial or at the appeal the alleged words or signs used by Mrs.Myatt to Beamish were first uttered, "We want truth. My boss wants truth. Will you tell us the truth because we have clever staff," pointing across to central Police Station. Much of this was made in the trial and during the appeal as to 'prove' that Beamish was formally cautioned, and that his subsequent alleged confessions were admissible as evidence.

But were they really?

Let us visualise a car. It has two seats in the front, and a long seat in the rear. We already know, because the evidence was not disputed, that there were five people in the car - Beamish himself, Leitch, Myatt, Deering and a police driver. The question that was never answered was where each person was sitting when this all took place. Obviously, the driver sat in the front right-hand seat behind the wheel, but where was Deering?

In evidence, Beamish stated that both Mrs.Myatt and Leitch were either poking him, pushing him, or waving a fist in his face, therefore Deering must have sat in the front passenger seat. This leaves Mrs.Myatt, Leitch and Beamish who all must have been in the back seat, and where was Beamish seated in relation to the other two? Obviously he was in the middle with Mrs.Myatt and Leitch on either side of him - the police were not going to be so stupid as to put Beamish beside a door which he could open and thus run away.

Right then, now remember Beamish was Deaf so he had to *look* at people to know what they were saying, so with Mrs.Myatt on one side allegedly pushing him, and Leitch on the other allegedly poking him and waving a fist under his nose, Beamish's head would be swivelling left and right all the time trying to understand what was going on. Let the reader imagine she or he is sitting atop of a tennis court net where a doubles is playing, so the ball is going to and fro across the net regularly so the reader has to swivel his or her head to and fro to watch it, and at the same time is being pushed and poked by two players who want him or her off the net.

And they try to make out that they delivered a 'warning' across to Beamish under those circumstances, and got a 'confession' out of him?

If that is not intimidation as alleged by Athol Gibson, and refuted by the trial judge and three appeal court judges, then what is it?

A cleverer lawyer than Athol Gibson with a greater degree of Deaf Awareness would have tied up the witnesses in knots in court trying to explain away these circumstances, and rendered the 'confession' inadmissible evidence. But nowhere in the trial did the defence pursue this strange setting.

Clearly, Chief Justice Wolff formed the view that Beamish's real defence was that the police and the interpreters had, in effect, 'fitted him up' with the murder charge, and he therefore asked the jury whether they found it possible to really believe that such conduct could have occurred on the part of people who of an apparently high character and reputation. The result was that the Chief Justice's attention in his summing up was focused on this point rather than the unquestionable fact that many of the answers were obtained from Beamish only after false starts resulting inevitably in some form of suggested answers, whether by Detective Sergeant Leitch or Mrs. Florence Myatt, which bore some resemblance to what these two people hoped to be the truth. Chief Justice Wolff therefore failed in his summing up to show his appreciation of the deficiencies in the strength of the evidence against Beamish resulting from the way the interrogation had been conducted, and to distinguish between the clear discrepancies between many matters stated by Beamish and the proven facts.

Chief Justice Wolff saw only what he wanted to see from the evidence in his summing up, just as Leitch and Mrs Myatt had only suggested to Beamish - with some apparent intimidation and bullying - what they wanted to discover from the interrogations. All this was compounded by some misdirected questioning by an inexperienced junior counsel during the trial. It was therefore not surprising that the jury convicted.

An appeal against the conviction was taken up before the Court of Criminal Appeal of Western Australia on 19,20 and 21 September before Messrs. Justices Jackson, Virtue and D'Arcy. This time, the defence added to their team a highly regarded Queen's Counsel, Mr.F.T.P.Burt.

The main ground of the appeal was that the trial judge should not have admitted the confessions of Beamish in evidence. There was also complaint of misdirection as to the burden of proof, and some criticism of the summing up. After the hearing, the three judges reserved judgement which was submitted on 20th October. In this judgement,

Mr. Justice Jackson confined himself to the questions of law that had been raised. Mr. Justice Virtue discussed the evidence in considerable detail and concluded it led to a strong inference of guilt. Mr. Justice D'Arcy also dealt mainly with the question of law. All three gave weight to Mrs. Myatt's words which although was not perhaps the accepted format of a given warning, they felt it was sufficient under the circumstances for a person like Beamish. They also gave weight to the character reference of Mrs. Myatt which had come from one of the defence witnesses.

It is of significance that both Justices Virtue and D'Arcy, in discussing the criticisms made of the summing up, agreed there were strong discrepancies between Beamish's statements and the known facts which Chief Justice Wolff had failed to mention to the jury. They were satisfied, however, that the jury's attention to these problems had been sufficiently captured during the taking of evidence and in speeches of counsel.

The appeal was dismissed, and the death sentence reaffirmed. An application for leave to appeal to the High Court of Australia was subsequently refused but the Government of Western Australia commuted the sentence of death for one of imprisonment with hard labour for life.

VII

And that should have been that. But the story was not quite over.

PART TWO

VIII

In the early hours of the summer night of 27 January 1963, several seemingly unrelated shootings took place across Perth, in what are now known as 'spree killings'. Nicholas August, a poultry dealer and a married man, was out sitting in a car sharing a drink with Ocean Beach barmaid, Rowena Reeves, when at around 2 a.m., the girl saw a man.
Thinking him a peeping Tom, August told him to 'bugger off', but the silent figure did not move, so August threw an empty beer bottle at him.
"Look out!" Rowena screamed. "He's got a gun!"
The man raised his rifle and took careful aim at August's head. At the last moment, Rowena pushed her companion's head down and the bullet nicked his neck, which began to bleed profusely.
"Start the car! Start the car!" the girl was yelling at August hysterically.
By the time August had reached the hospital, the girl was unconscious. The bullet which had nicked August's neck had also struck the girl in the arm.
Both Nicholas August and Rowena Reeves survived, but others were not so lucky that night.
Just over an hour later and a couple of miles away, 54-year old retired grocer, George Walmsley, answered some very persistent ringing of his doorbell, and was shot immediately he opened the front door. The bullet hit him in the forehead, and he was dead by the time his wife and

daughter, both shaken wide awake by the gunshot, had got downstairs.

A little while later around the corner at Mrs. Allen's boarding house, a student named Scott McWilliam from the University of Western Australia was awoken by Mrs. Allen's niece, Pauline, shaking his shoulder.

"There's something wrong with John," she said, referring to a 19-year old fellow University student named John Sturkey who had been sleeping out on the verandah in the heat of the Australian night.

McWilliam went out onto the verandah, and heard strange noises coming from Sturkey's throat. McWilliam raised Sturkey's head. There was a bullet hole between his eyes. John Sturkey was dead by the time the police and ambulance arrived.

Next morning, a man named Brian Weir who lived in nearby Broome Street, did not show up for training at the Surf Lifesaving Club, so one of the crew was sent round to get him out of bed.

The crew member found him in his bed with a bullet wound in his forehead and serious brain damage. Brian Weir died from his wounds three years later.

A few days later, a young women named Rosemary Anderson, aged 17, was run down by a car and pronounced dead on arrival at hospital.

Then, on the morning of 16 February, Joy Noble was up early making breakfast when she looked out of the window of her West Perth home and saw spread-eagled on her lawn the naked body of a young woman. At first Joy Noble thought it was her daughter, and she ran through the house shouting "Carline!."

In fact, the woman, Constance Lucy Maddrill, a 24 year-old social worker, lived next door. She had been strangled and raped, probably in the early hours of the morning while her flatmate, Jennifer Hurst, slept, and her body dragged out of the flat to be dumped on the lawn next door where further perverted sexual acts were carried out, probably after death. When found, her *left arm had been carefully wrapped* around an empty whisky bottle, a symbolic thing which left police investigators puzzled. No-one could also explain why the attacker had dragged her all the way over to the Nobles' lawn then abandoned her. Because of this, and the symbolic whisky bottle, the police thought an Aborigine had done it, even though there were no records of aborigines attacking white girls in Western Australia. The police certainly felt this murder had nothing to do with the shooting spree three weeks earlier.

These shooting and murder sprees plunged the city of Perth into terror, whilst the police tried vainly to find the person or persons responsible, and the local press offered a thousand pounds as a reward for the capture of the 'Maniac Slayer', as the spree killer was dubbed.

No-one was sure whether the killings and shootings were all connected or not, and the police evidently decided that the murder of Rosemary Anderson was not connected with the other killings by arresting a young man named Button for the murder, and he was subsequently sentenced to ten years hard labour for this crime.

Throughout the next few months, however, five other young women were to report that they had been victims of hit-and-run incidents. They were convinced that someone had tried to run them down on purpose. In the same period, three other young women were seriously assaulted and raped.

Finally, on a thundery night on 10th August 1963, an eighteen year-old science student at the University of Western Australia was baby-sitting Carl and Wendy Dowds' eight-month-old son, Mitchell, whilst the Dowdses were out at a party. On their return from their party, the Dowdses found their baby-sitter slumped on the sofa with a peaceful look on her face like she had just fallen asleep. She had been shot with a .22 rifle and she was quite dead. Baby Mitchell was unharmed. There could be no doubt that this killing was linked with the murders in January.

Perth experienced mass panic. The *West Australian* advised people to lock their doors at night - unheard of in Perth at that time. Baby-sitters were warned not to sit near windows, and there were proposals to close the old alleyways that ran down the back of people's houses. The police in desperation called in the assistance of Scotland Yard and the United States' F.B.I.

However, by a stroke of extreme good fortune, an elderly couple out picking flowers in Mount Pleasant accidentally discovered a rifle hidden in some bushes behind a rock, and called in the police. Tests proved that the rifle had been the same one that had killed John Sturkey, George Walmsley and Shirley McLeod and also the one used in the other shootings. Police returned the gun to its hiding place, and lay in wait to see if it would be recovered by the killer. Their luck paid off on 1st September 1963 when a Perth truck driver and known burglar named Eric Edgar Cooke returned to the hiding place to retrieve the gun, and was arrested by police without a struggle.

At the time of his arrest, he was in possession of a pair of black ladies briefs in his pocket, and was wearing a pair of white ladies gloves.

Cooke had at the time of his arrest burgled some 250 houses, and had spent three short terms in prison before his arrest by the police as a suspect in the murder of Shirley McLeod.

At the police station, Cooke was charged with the murder of Shirley McLeod, a charge which he initially denied by claiming he was at home on the night the girl was killed, but confessed when his wife told police he had not been home.

He was naturally interrogated extensively in Central police station with regard to the other 1963 killings, and taken to the scene of the Lucy Maddrill murder. Cooke told police he had been robbing the two girls' flat when he had knocked over a photograph in Lucy Maddrill's bedroom. She had woken up, and tried to scream, but Cooke hit her first, and throttled her. He dragged her into the next bedroom, strangled her with a lamp flex and then raped her. He had intended to hide the body, and had dragged it outside and left it on the Nobles' lawn while he looked for a car to steal. However, he could not find one, and stole a bicycle instead, using it to ride home. (Cooke was not actually charged with this offence until 25th October 1963).

Two days after his arrest, on 3rd September, Cooke was additionally charged with the murders of John Sturkey and George Walmsley, and the shootings of Brian Weir, Nicholas August and Rowena Reeves. He confessed he had shot five people because he 'wanted to hurt somebody'.

Out on his usual Saturday night prowl looking for houses to burgle, he had stolen a Lithgow single-shot .22 and a tan-coloured Holden sedan. He had been driving aimlessly when he saw a man and a woman in a parked car. The interior light went out so Cooke thought he would stop the car and spy on the couple. He took the rifle with him, so when the couple spotted him and threw a bottle at him, he shot back.

Driving on to Broome Street, he decided to do a bit more burglary, and stopped by a house to clamber over some railings up to a balcony where there were some french windows. However, Cooke found that there was a man sleeping on a bed inside the french windows preventing him from getting into the house, so he shot at the sleeping body. The result was that Brian Weir suffered irreversible brain damage leading to his death three years later.

Continuing to prowl around the block, Cooke found a man sleeping on a verandah. Another shot from the .22 rifle ended young John Sturkey's life.

The next killing was even more deliberate and callous. In Louise Street, he picked a house at random, leant the rifle against the garage wall, and went to ring the front door bell continuously. When Cooke heard sounds from inside the house that the irritated owner was coming to answer the door, he ran back to the rifle, levelled the gun, and let George Walmsley have it directly between the eyes. He then drove off in the Holden, returning it to the house from which he had stolen it. The owner noticed the next morning it was parked differently, and that the interior light had been removed, but had felt the matter too petty to bother the police about.

He also admitted to police interrogators that he had previously stabbed and killed a woman a few years earlier when his fourth child, his eldest daughter - one of twins - was born seriously disabled. It had a cleft palate, and a stump where its right arm had been, and in his anger at the latest injustice to blighten his life, Cooke had left the hospital in a rage and ended up killing this woman. A check with the date of birth of the twins showed that it had been born on the day before the body of Pnina Berkman was found murdered in her South Perth flat in January 1959!

This was, it must be remembered, a murder that the police had always believed was linked with that of Jillian Brewer!

If alarm bells were not already ringing throughout Perth Central police station, they should have been!

IX

Eric Edgar Cooke, who was 31 years of age at the time of his arrest, was small in stature and a social misfit who had been born with a hare-lip and a cleft palate, and had grown up a sickly child who did not please his father, who frequently gave him beatings. He hated his father, especially after he had spent three weeks in hospital trying to protect his mother from one of his father's onslaughts. At school, his smallness, ugly rasping voice and distorted face made him the target of taunts and bullying. One day, when several boys set upon him and rubbed his face in the sand, he vowed he would get his revenge against all of them.

He became a delinquent at an early age, and after he had been expelled from several schools, he quit completely at age fourteen. The petty offences became more frequent and more serious. As a youth, he burned with resentment as pretty girls he had watched with envy turned their eyes away from him in embarrassment. At night, he prowled the city and the suburbs alone, light-footed and silent, preferring the darkness. His frustrated sexual ambitions led him to become a peeping tom, peering into bedroom windows or at cuddling couples in parked cars.

He learnt to break skilfully into houses and steal while unsuspecting occupants were in the next room, to push cars noiselessly out of garages and start them with pieces of wire, but all that was not enough. He had an urge to destroy, and after being rejected by the Church as a member of the choir or as a Sunday School teacher, and took out his revenge on another church miles away which he set alight and sat in a bus watching it burn to the ground. A series of other arson attacks followed, including the burning down of a theatre. Fortunately, no-one was ever killed in his arson activities, but when police caught up with him, they realised they had upon their hands a young man with an explosive mixture of emotions, hates and sexual problems. He was sent to gaol for 18 months for the arson activities, but it did not cure him. He was in more trouble after his release but it only led him to become more skilful and cunning in his nocturnal roamings.

Cooke got a job in the Perth fruit and vegetable market centre where he met a girl who for the first time gave him the love and affection he needed. After a brief courtship, they married, and Cooke settled down for the only brief period of happiness he had in his life.

This happiness seemed complete when their first son was born, but Cooke became bitter when it was found the boy had severe learning difficulties, but he promised to lavish it with the love and care he had lacked as a child. Two further children were born to Eric and Sally Cooke over the next few years. Both were normal, and to neighbours, the Cookes were a happy couple, devoted to their family especially the mentally retarded first-born. Eric was popular and cheerful, with his job as a truck driver, always willing to do everyone a good turn even if he was often out late at night.

It was the birth of his eldest daughter with its cleft palate, distorted face like himself, with a stump for an arm into the bargain, that sent Cooke over the edge to take impersonal but terrible revenge against society in general, and it was the unfortunate Pnina Berkman who became the first victim of his terrible revenge.

Sally Cooke confirmed to detectives later that she remembered her husband coming to visit her the day after the birth of their twin daughters with scratches on his face, which he had laughed off as having received by accident from one of his other children.

However, Cooke's admission at Perth Central police station of the Berkman murder caused police to subject him to even more intense questioning, and on 10 September, whilst remanded in custody, he was being interrogated by Detective Sergeant Nielson. In the same room as witnesses were Detective Sergeants Dunne and Moorman. Out of the blue, Cooke stated that he had been responsible for two crimes for which two other men were serving sentences of imprisonment. These were the murders of Jillian Brewer and Rosemary Anderson.

Stunned, Nielson and his colleagues abandoned questioning for the day, and after consulting between themselves, they decided to test Cooke on the Anderson killing for which the young man Button was serving a ten-year sentence.

The next day, they reconvened at Perth Central, and took Cooke to where he stated he had killed Rosemary Anderson, and took down his version of how he had killed her. They repeated the process the next day, where Cooke verified various positions on the roadway where Miss Anderson had been killed.

On their return to the police station, Cooke wrote out a full statement of this killing in his own handwriting. After studying this statement, the detectives told Cooke that his account of the Anderson killing did not appear to match some of the known facts. Cooke was then told that he could not have been responsible, and he then wrote out a retraction of his confession, again in his own handwriting.

The next day, 13th September, Nielson had summoned Detective Sergeant Leitch and requested he join him, Dunne and Moorman when they re-interviewed Cooke, this time about the murder of Jillian Brewer and asked him to give an account how he had done this. The account was given, and when it had ended, Nielson and Leitch held a conference outside the room. On their return, Nielson stated that Cooke's account was inconsistent with known facts of the killing, omitting in particular a number of blows which had been inflicted. Nielson told Cooke what these blows were.

Cooke then said he could see that he could not have committed this murder either, and he was then taken into the office of Inspector Lamb, Head of the Perth C.I.B., where he again stated he could not have been responsible for the killings of Jillian Brewer and Rosemary Anderson.

Cooke was then returned to Fremantle Gaol, and the police took no further action on the alleged statements and retractions by Cooke of the killings of Jillian Brewer and Rosemary Anderson, taking the view that he was making false confessions for his own ulterior motives.

There it might have remained but for a series of interviews that Cooke had with his solicitor (who was also his junior counsel). These two men were sometimes joined in these interviews by the senior counsel appointed to undertake the defence.

At an early stage in these interviews, Cooke told his counsel that he had mentioned to the police he had killed Jillian Brewer and Rosemary Anderson, and they had shown him he could not possibly have done so. He added he had read all about the cases and everything was so real in his mind he actually thought he had done the killings. A few days later, he reverted to the subject again and said he was in two minds about the Anderson murder and also about the Brewer killing, which he described in great detail to counsel. His attitude was that he thought he had killed Jillian Brewer but the police had told him he could not have done so.

In subsequent interviews, he stated he had given matters a lot of thought and he was positive he had killed both Miss Brewer and Miss Anderson.

The police got to hear something about Cooke's change of mind, because on 31 October, he was visited by the Reverend Prestage B.Sullivan who had known Cooke for 12 years and who had previously visited him in prison. Prior to this visit, Sullivan had a conversation with Detective Sergeant Dunne (who had been one of the police interrogators). The intention was that Sullivan would find out for Dunne what Cooke had been saying to his counsel. It is not known if Sullivan subsequently related to Dunne what had happened during his visit to Cooke - it would be a breach of professional ethics if he had, but then the question of professional ethics does not seem to have been a strong point either with the police, sign language interpreters or the judiciary around this time in Western Australia, and there is no reason why the clergy should be any different.

In his long conversation with Cooke, the latter said quite specifically that he had killed both Miss Anderson and Miss Brewer and that his reason for changing his earlier statement and denying the killings were that they were of such a nature he was ashamed of them. Cooke gave Sullivan a long and detailed account of the circumstances surrounding his alleged killing of Jillian Brewer.

Nothing more was done about Cooke's allegations of the killings of Rosemary Anderson and Jillian Brewer before he stood trial at the end of November 1963 on charge of the wilful murder of John Sturkey. The charges of wilful murder against Shirley McLeod and George Walmsley, and of Constance Lucy Maddrill and Pnina Berkman, which had only been added on 25 October were not tried. He was found guilty and sentenced to death by hanging.

X

With Cooke's trial out of the way, his counsel were now in a position to advise legal representatives for Beamish and Button of the allegations made by Cooke for which their clients were serving life sentences.

Accordingly, on 4 December 1963, a solicitor acting for Beamish held a long interview with Eric Cooke at Fremantle Gaol in the presence of the Deputy Superintendent of the prison.

In this interview, Cooke made an oral statement which was written down by the solicitor. Cooke then read and signed his name to each page of the statement, then swore out an affidavit witnessed by the Deputy Superintendent to the effect that all the facts in the statement were true and correct.

The Reverend Sullivan also swore out an affidavit that all the facts in the statement tallied with the facts that were in the oral statement made to him by Cooke on 31 October.

A private enquiry agent, a Mr.M.G.Blight, was shown a copy of Cooke's signed statement by Beamish's solicitor, and asked to investigate certain matters referred to in it which were capable of independent collaboration. On 17 December, the private enquiry agent swore out an affidavit detailing the result of his investigations.

Meanwhile, Beamish's legal advisers petitioned the Government of Western Australia for mercy on Beamish's behalf, and requested that the Minister of Justice should refer the matter to the Supreme Court of Western Australia for consideration. This was done by the Minister on 4 February 1964.

The result of the Minister's action was to give the Court of Criminal Appeal of Western Australia power to give consideration to the matter in the same manner as if Beamish was bringing in an ordinary appeal. Under its powers of hearing ordinary or regular appeals, the court could receive fresh evidence and it was, of course, invited to exercise this power by receiving the evidence of Cooke's confessions.

A similar petition was lodged and granted on behalf of the young man Button.

The Court of Criminal Appeal convened to hear the Minister's reference on the Beamish case - hereafter called the second appeal - on 27 February 1964. Beamish was represented by the same Queen's Counsel as had appeared for him in the first appeal, Mr. F.T.P.Burt, Q.C.

The 27 February hearing was essentially to decide upon procedure, and the appeal proper was heard on 17, 18, 19 and 20 March 1964. The first two days were devoted to argument from counsel on both sides on both legal and factual aspects of the case, then on the third day, several witnesses who had sworn out affidavits for the Crown were cross-examined by Beamish's counsel. Finally, on 20 March, Eric Edgar Cooke was brought to the court and cross-examined by the Crown Prosecutor, after which Beamish's counsel made a brief concluding speech.

The court reserved their consideration of the matter, and on 22 May, delivered their judgements dismissing Beamish's appeal.

An application for special leave to appeal to the High Court of Australia, a superior court to the courts of Western Australia, was dismissed after a very brief hearing. No written judgements were delivered.

A further application on Beamish's behalf was made to the Privy Council for special leave to appeal, but again was dismissed after a brief hearing.

This was an appalling abuse of judicial powers.

XI

Eric Edgar Cooke was hanged at Fremantle Gaol on 26th October 1964 for the murder of John Sturkey, and the chance of hearing his evidence in a proper court to correct a serious miscarriage of justice not only to Beamish but also to Button was lost forever.

XII

We now need to look at the circumstances surrounding the belief that there had been a serious miscarriage of injustice in the two cases of Beamish and Button. There are three questions that need to be asked.

The first question to be asked is - was anybody going to admit they had got it all wrong the first time round?

The second question - did Beamish receive a fair hearing in his second appeal?

The third question - was there any independent evidence that could collaborate Cooke's statements and allegations that he was the person responsible for the murders of Jillian Brewer and Rosemary Anderson?

The first and second questions are so closely interwoven together that they will be examined and dealt with as one question.

XIII

We have previously looked at the role of Mrs.Myatt earlier in this story, the way she misused her position as so-called interpreter, and since she did not play any part in the appeals, we will leave it at that, and turn to Detective Sergeant George O. Leitch.

It comes across in the original trial evidence and from other sources that Leitch was an "aggressive" character, and there seems to be little doubt that he did intimidate and bully Beamish so thoroughly that Beamish was more than anxious to **any** suggestion put forward either by Leitch or Mrs.Myatt that this or that circumstance happened, with the result that the police ended up with an alleged confession or statement which Chief Justice Wolff admitted into evidence despite objections from junior counsel Athol Gibson.

It will be recalled that Leitch was not part of the original team who interrogated Cooke, and was called in by Detective Sergeant Nielson on **only one occasion** to hear what Cooke had to say about Jillian Brewer's murder. It will also be recalled that after this confession by Cooke, Sergeants Leitch and Nielson had a conference by themselves outside the room, after which Nielson returned to the interview room and informed Cooke he could not have done the murder.

Does anyone honestly believe that Leitch was going to admit that he had been wrong with the conviction of Beamish, and possibly open himself and the police to charges of false imprisonment and abuse of civil rights?

Of course not!

It is therefore not surprising that Nielson got Cooke to retract his confession.

Another interesting point in connection with this is that whereas Cooke actually wrote out a statement and a subsequent retraction in his own handwriting regarding the murder of Rosemary Anderson, no such written statement or retraction by Cooke was ever admitted to having been written regarding the murder of Jillian Brewer for the time that Leitch was part of the team with Detective Sergeants Nielson, Dunne and Moorman. In view of the statements elicited from Leitch by Athol Gibson at the original trial that he had "destroyed" pieces of paper which the defence regarded as essential to their case as proof that Beamish did not kill Jillian Brewer, this in itself is highly suspicious of a cover up either by Leitch alone, or in concert with others.

Let us now move on to the second appeal, and see who was sitting on the panel of judges hearing the appeal, and subsequently dismissing it.

Chief Justice Wolff!!

Who was the trial judge and who had been criticised for his biased summing up at the original trial!

Mr. Justices Jackson and Virtue!!

Who had heard the first Beamish appeal!

It is difficult to understand how the Chief Justice, on whom lay responsibility for allocating the judicial work before his court, could have allowed this farcical situation to happen.

In the second appeal, the Court of Criminal Appeal was being asked to decide whether a miscarriage of justice might have occurred. If there had, then the very judges who had either tried the case in the first place, or heard an earlier appeal and dismissed that appeal, were inescapably involved in that miscarriage of justice. No man of honour and integrity would willingly contemplate that he had participated in condemning an innocent man to life imprisonment, particularly a man as helpless as Beamish due to his communication problems.

It is an axiom of Anglo-Saxon law that justice must not only be done but be seen to be done. No judge should therefore participate in an appeal against his own decision in a previous hearing.

At the time of the second appeal, there were seven justices constituting the Supreme Court of Western Australia, and three of them (the fourth was Mr. Justice D'Arcy) had not been involved in the earlier proceedings, therefore it should have been commonsense for the Chief Justice to roster these three judges to hear the second appeal. If for some reason, these three judges could not be available, then it should have been reported to the Minister of Justice who had referred the case to the court that a properly-constituted and impartial court could not be assembled and a request made to him to appoint Commissioners, possibly from outside Western Australia.

Beamish, and his counsel, were in an almost impossible position. The Q.C., Burt, made no attempt to object to the constitution of the court. If he had, and failed, there would have been the risk that his client's case would be severely prejudiced in the eyes of men who had their supposed impartiality and honour questioned.

The second appeal therefore took place in front of three judges who may have gone into it with already-formed opinions instead of open minds.

For instance, Chief Justice Wolff might be said to have formed an opinion from the original trial that witnesses against Beamish were telling the truth. This is clear from the report delivered to the first Court of Criminal Appeal by the Chief Justice on the question of evidence given by Sergeant Leitch and Mrs. Myatt.

It might also be said that Mr. Justice Virtue had stated in his judgement in the first appeal that he had great difficulty in seeing how Beamish had become aware of some of the details of the crime unless he had done it, or else had the details suggested to him or been the result of some inspired guesswork. In his view, it was highly improbable that Beamish had come across the details through suggestion or guesswork, and therefore he must be guilty.

It might also be said that Mr. Justice Jackson, in the first appeal, had stated how impressed he was by the scrupulous care taken by Leitch in his dealings with Beamish.

On the other hand, it might be said that these prior impressions held by the three judges could be corrected by satisfactory evidence from Cooke.

In reality, it was not until the court delivered its reasons for dismissing the second appeal that it became clear how strong previously held impressions by two of the three judges had influenced their rejection of the appeal.

Chief Justice Wolff's analysis of the evidence against Beamish concludes that the case against him was 'of great probative strength.' He had seen nothing to change his opinion of Beamish since the first trial.

Mr. Justice Virtue goes even further by stating that as appellate judge in the first appeal, he had then formed the opinion the case against Beamish was a very strong one indeed, and that in hearing previous cases against Cooke, he had then formed the opinion that he was a 'palpable and unscrupulous liar.' He had therefore seen no reason to change his previously held opinions.

Only Mr. Justice Jackson seems to have tried to be fair, and in his judgement, he expressed some doubts and anxieties which escaped his partners on the bench.

For counsel for Beamish, the difficulties were formidable, but there was even more. He was faced with a complete lack of understanding by three judges as to the correct procedures for judges in appeal courts. Where fresh evidence is tendered in a court of appeal that had not been available in the original trial, it is not the function of the judges to act as jury in respect of this fresh evidence or that they accept it. It is their function to decide whether this evidence could be influential to a jury in reaching a verdict, and if this was the case, their duty was to order a re-trial or quash the conviction. Instead, the second Court of Criminal Appeal took it upon themselves to re-try the case against Beamish.

This was a serious misuse of judicial powers and a serious miscarriage of justice by men who ought to have known better.

XIV

As for the third question - was there any independent evidence which could be shown to collaborate either Beamish's or Cooke's statements for the murder of Jillian Brewer?

There was.

These were, respectively, the milk bottle and the frying pan.

In respect of Beamish, the case against him rested upon his alleged statements alone. There was no other evidence to link him with the murder, except that he knew Brookwood Flats but this is easily explained by his friendship with Susanne Delaney, and in any case Miss Delaney did not start living at Brookwood Flats before November 1960.

With Cooke, however, there was other evidence to link him with his presence at Brookwood Flats on the night of 19/20 December 1959 when Jillian Brewer was murdered. Let us take the milk bottle first.

In his lengthy statement to Beamish's solicitor on 4 December 1963, Cooke described in detail how he had gained entry into the Brewer flat and stated, without any prompting, that he had seen two milkmen doing their rounds, and had stolen a bottle of milk from their van and drunk it. After the milkmen had gone, he had entered the Brewer flat through the back door at about 2.45 a.m., and that just inside the door he had found a one-third pint milk bottle which had apparently just been delivered in the usual way, through the flap in the door. Later in his statement, Cooke had said that between his attacks on Jillian Brewer, he had used the milk bottle to prop open the door while he was going in and out of the flat.

Nowhere in his statement to the police did Beamish make any mention of the milk bottle, and there was a statement by the milkman to the effect that he usually delivered the milk between 4 a.m. and 5 a.m. but that particular night he had reversed his round and had delivered the milk between 2 a.m. and 2.15 a.m., and that he had met up with another milkman during that part of his round.

This was collaborative evidence obtained independently which tallied with Cooke's statement, and it was something that Cooke could never have known unless he had been there at the time he said he was.

In the second appeal, Mr. Justice Jackson said that it was a 'startling coincidence', and dismissed the evidence as worthless!

The frying pan incident was of similar significance. It will be recalled that the Jillian Brewer crime scene was extensively photographed before the arrival of the police pathologist at 10.30 a.m. Many of these photographs were never submitted into trial evidence, and had remained in police files. Certainly, they had never been issued to any newspapers. They had not even been seen by Beamish's defence team until much later, when they asked for the full files for the second appeal.

In his sworn statement, Cooke had stated that when he had walked into the kitchenette, he had seen an electric frying pan on the draining section of the sink.

Cooke could never have known that among the photographs taken on the discovery of the murder made available to the defence by the police, there was a photograph of the kitchenette which clearly showed an electric frying pan standing almost exactly where Cooke said he had seen it. This photograph had never been used during the trial or the first appeal.

Again, Mr. Justice Jackson was not impressed by the evidence of the frying pan, thinking that Cooke could have been in the flat on another occasion and seen it then.

Mr. Justice Virtue thought the two matters 'rather surprising coincidences' and was possibly swayed by the comment of the Crown Prosecutor that :

> "even if Cooke was in the flat some time after 2.30 a.m. or later on the night in question, it would not be the most remarkable thing in the world. You have got two prowlers out in one night, in the same area and in succession, they are in the same premises."

Two prowlers ?
Perhaps.
Two sadistic murderers?

In the same area and the same flat?
On the same night?
In a city like Perth?
That was stretching coincidences a bit too far.
In any case, it was not really the function of the three justices hearing the second appeal to act as jury on this type of evidence. Their function was to consider whether, if this type of evidence had been known to the jury at the trial, Beamish would have been convicted as he had been.
Throughout the second appeal judgements, the three justices made great play of dissecting any apparent discrepancies in Cooke's statements, and branding them untruthful, yet at the same time, holding up Beamish's statements which also contained some discrepancies as truthful, putting these discrepancies down to the 'difficulties in interpreting'.
In particular, the Chief Justice took great care to draw attention to Beamish's allegations at his trial that he had been intimidated by Detective Sergeant Leitch, Mrs. Myatt and the Reverend Chetwynd and to say emphasise once again how strong the personal characters of these people were, therefore Beamish's defence was fabricated.
There was one other area of great importance where the three justices seemed to totally ignore. It was the blow to the windpipe which Dr.Pearson in his evidence during the trial stated was the primary cause of death. Nowhere in his statement did Beamish ever allude to delivering the blow to the throat, neither did Cooke.
However, with Beamish, the three justices inferred that he was in such a frenzy of killing that he could not remember the precise sequence of hits, yet with Cooke, they took the line that his absence of stating he had struck a blow to the throat showed that he was fabricating his story!

In his actual judgement Chief Justice Wolff actually says:

> "One of the most incredible statements concerning the killing of Brewer as described by Cooke is the detail which he gives of going out of the flat to dispose of the hatchet, suspending operations during the killing. At this time Brewer had received severe wounds on the scalp which must have rendered her unconscious. After a lapse of time, Cooke says he returned and set about stabbing her with the scissors. Describing the girl he says in lying detail : 'Every breath she took made a rattling noise in her throat and she woke and said 'who is it' in a very slow manner. It is clear from his description of when he got the scissors that he must have already chopped through the windpipe with the hatchet before he got the scissors."

His use of the phrases 'most incredible' and 'lying detail' shows clearly what views the Chief Justice had of Cooke's evidence.

Yet, in answer to questions put to him in parliament, the Prime Minister of Western Australia revealed on 21 October (five days before Cooke was hanged) that an officer of the Crown Law Department had sought advice on Cooke's claim that Jillian Brewer had spoken a few words in his presence before dying, and the advice received that it would be improbable but not impossible. He revealed that the advice was given to the police but was not put to the court. This shows that the police and the Crown Law Department knew before the second appeal hearing that it was 'not impossible' that Jillian Brewer had spoken in the way Cooke said she had, but the Crown prosecutor was totally unaware of that fact and therefore quite unwittingly led the court into an error on a matter to which at least two of its members regarded of utmost importance, and the matter remained uncorrected when the subsequent High Court of Australia dismissed Beamish's special appeal of leave.

If this episode had occurred, for example, in a United States court, its judgement would probably have been quashed and the case sent for re-trial on the grounds there had not been a fair hearing. On that re-trial, the jury could have heard Cooke give evidence (as well as all the evidence against Beamish) and they could have decided whether there was reasonable doubt of Beamish's guilt. The respective records of Darryl Beamish and Eric Edgar Cooke make it far more likely that it was Cooke who killed Jillian Brewer. It was surely significant that the police accepted Cooke had killed Pnina Berkman yet at the time of the Brewer murder, they were so utterly convinced the same man had killed both Berkman and Brewer.

Darryl Beamish might have been a paedophile with a liking for interfering with little girls, but it did not automatically follow that he would switch his sexual tastes to older women. We have Susanne Delaney's evidence that in all their time together, Beamish never so much as touched her, never mind kiss her.

But it was too late for any re-trial to happen - Cooke had been hanged!

There was another matter revealed in parliament which does not seem to have been known to Beamish's advisers (nor for that matter, Button's advisers) and it seemed also to have been withheld from the court.

The police had accepted as fact Cooke's claim to unlawfully wounding a woman and a man, to sexually assaulting three other women causing them actual bodily harm, and to committing over twenty offences of burglary. They had also accepted as fact his statement that he *"liked to drive around at night to catch any girl out walking, then drive my car at them to hurt them."* The police accepted that he had injured five women in this manner.

Cooke's confession to the killing of Rosemary Anderson by running her down with a car might not seem so incredible if the jury in Button's trial had known of the claims to five other similar crimes. At the very least, they would have had serious doubts of the prosecution case against Button and would very probably have acquainted him.

XV - Postscript

A few minutes before he stepped onto the scaffold to be hanged, Cooke repeated to a minister of religion his responsibility for the murder of Jillian Brewer, and to the Superintendent of Fremantle Gaol, his responsibility for 'the other two murders'.

There was no reason for him to make these statements. He was about to die anyway.

Darryl Beamish remained in Fremantle Gaol until his parole in 1971. He has never been pardoned for the Brewer crime, and has never been compensated for his miscarriage of justice (Indeed, it is not regarded as such by Western Australia).

It is generally accepted these days that it is unsafe to convict anyone solely on their own confession, as Beamish was. The recent British cases of *the Birmingham*

Six, the Bridgewater Four and the *Guildford Four* highlight only too clearly the dangers of relying on unsafe evidence. It may be time to set the record straight and obtain justice for Beamish.

Note : The author has not studied trial records of the Rosemary Anderson case, which resulted in the conviction of the man named Button, and he does not know what happened to Button, although it is clear that according to one source that in 1965, Button was still in prison therefore it is likely that Button served his time and was accorded as great a miscarriage of injustice as Beamish suffered.

6.   1988 : Waitotara, New Zealand

THE LONG ARREST

Waitotara in the North Island of New Zealand is typical of many rural communities in that country. The nearest large city is Wanganui, approximately 20 miles to the east, where the nearest police headquarters is based. Waitotara itself was too small to have a police station of its own.

Situated near the mouth of the river of the same name, Waitotara sits on the main road, and the railway line, between Wanganui and New Plymouth approximately 70 miles to the west. There are a few houses, a few farms, many spread out some distance apart from each other. It also had a school-house, and just one general store.

It was to this store that two sisters set out one fine morning, 5th October 1988, to do some shopping. They left behind in the house one of the sister's husband to baby-sit a fifteen-month old baby which was asleep in its cot.

What happened when the two sisters returned to the house from the general store after being away about 25 minutes was to led to one of New Zealand's most controversial prosecutions.

The first indication that anything was wrong was reported to Wanganui police headquarters on the morning of 6th October.

A pathologist at Wanganui Hospital, Dr. Samuel Chan, reported to the police that he had just completed a post mortem examination on the body of a 15 month-old baby boy. He reported that death had resulted from internal bleeding caused by damage to the baby's heart. There was also damage to the liver, and the body also had four broken ribs. Knuckle marks were evident on the baby's chest, consistent with a blow being delivered to the chest. Dr. Chan estimated that there had been two or three blows required to have caused the injuries he had found on the baby's body.

The circumstances of the death of the infant seemed suspicious enough to warrant a homicide investigation, and the despatch of a police detachment under the command of Detective Senior Sergeant Scott. He was accompanied by a Detective Cunningham and a Constable Kerrisk, a 26 year-old uniformed branch police officer who was on secondment to the Criminal Investigation Branch. Making up the team was a Detective Constable Harrod.

The circumstances of the team's briefing and departure for Waitotara, and the handling of the police investigation that followed were to be the subject of considerable debate and controversy in the months that followed, culminating in a severely critical documentary broadcast on Television-New Zealand1 in 1992, leading to a police complaints authority investigation.

Basically, this boiled down to whether the investigating team knew they were going to interview a Deaf person, and what preparations - if any - they had made to conduct such an interview, as well as the circumstances of the actual interview itself.

The inclusion of Detective Constable Harrod in the police detachment going to Waitotara on the afternoon of 6th October presupposes that the team was aware that a Deaf person had to be interviewed. Harrod had previous dealings with the person in question and was fully aware that he was Deaf. Moreover, Harrod also knew that the person about to be interviewed could not read or write

English, and that he relied on sign language to communicate.

Detective Senior Sergeant Scott, in charge of the detachment, denied that he had ever been briefed back at police headquarters prior to their departure that he had been told the team was to interview a Deaf person.

On the other hand, Constable Kerrisk who was the person that Scott deployed to question the Deaf person, was firm in his opinion that he had known before he got to Waitotara that the person he was about to interview had "some hearing disabilities".

However, he had been sitting in the back of the police car with Detective Constable Harrod during the journey to Waitotara, and it is possible that it was Harrod himself (perhaps peeved that it was Kerrisk who was to do the interviewing) that told him of the person's "hearing difficulties" without being overheard by Scott or Cunningham sitting in the front of the car.

Unfortunately, Detective Constable Harrod was to die within months of the Waitotara investigation, long before the police complaints authority investigation got under way, so no-one was able to question him.

The person they were going to see was a 21 year-old man named Ivan Curry who lived with his wife Whetu and sister-in-law Raeone Wirihana-Tawake in a house situated in Waitotara. Also living with them was a 15 month-old boy named Hauata Wirihana-Tawake, the son of Raeone. Commonly referred to as Sandy, the child had died under suspicious circumstances the previous day, the morning of 5th October.

On that morning, Ivan Curry had been alone in the house with his nephew who was asleep in his cot whilst the two sisters had gone out for a short while to the general store for a bit of shopping. It was alleged that when the two women returned from the store, they had found Sandy dead and Ivan in a panic. There was no accurate indication of how the child had died, or how long the two women had been absent from the house.

The police team arrived in Waitotara shortly after 3 p.m., and only then did Constable Kerrisk realise he needed expert assistance to communicate with Ivan Curry, and telephoned police headquarters in Wanganui to try and obtain the services of someone able to communicate in sign language to assist in the investigation.

Owing to the lack of an appropriate venue to conduct interviews in Waitotara, the police requested and were given the facilities of the school at Waitotara, and it was there that Ivan Curry and the two sisters were taken to be interviewed and their statements taken.

The first interview of Ivan Curry began at about 3.35 p.m. and was conducted by Constable Kerrisk communicating himself with Ivan without any professional assistance such as that of a sign language expert. Kerrisk, who had previously never had any contact with a Deaf sign language user, employed all sorts of methods to communicate with Ivan Curry - with pen and paper, by shouting (as people who are not deaf-aware tend to do), and by gesture.

For most of the time, the two of them were allegedly alone in the schoolroom although Detective Senior Sergeant Scott was alleged to have looked in from time to time. As the interview seemed to be progressing satisfactorily, the senior police officer saw no reason to interfere.

Kerrisk himself told the police complaints authority investigation that his interview was being supervised by Detective Cunningham who, however, did not say anything during the course of the interview.

Kerrisk adopted the procedure of recording the answers of Ivan Curry to questions that were put to him. The record of the answers suggested that there was some meaningful communication between the officer and the suspect, including admissions from Curry that he had punched Sandy Tawake three times in the chest.

Ivan Curry later denied that he had ever said that he had punched the child at all, never mind three times. He alleged that at one stage during the interview, one of the police officers had attempted to strike him, but he had ducked and the blow had missed. He described the officer delivering the blow as having a moustache, which pointed to Sergeant Scott as he was the only one with a moustache.

During the complaints investigation, Detective Senior Sergeant Scott and Constable Kerrisk denied that any officer had verbally or physically threatened Ivan Curry.

The first interview with Ivan Curry at Waitotara schoolhouse was terminated at 4.59 p.m., and Curry was taken to Wanganui police headquarters for further questioning.

The procedures adopted for the interviews at Waitotara school, particularly the deployment of Constable Kerrisk to interview Ivan Curry, on the afternoon of 6th October 1988 were one of the central criticisms of police conduct highlighted in the television documentary, which also called into question the conduct and competence of Detective Senior Sergeant Scott and encompassed the issue whether Ivan Curry should have faced trial at all.

At the time of the interview, Constable Kerrisk had been in the police force for seven years and had been seconded to the Criminal Investigation Branch for six months on mainly enquiry work, during which he had conducted a detective's induction course just prior to interviewing Ivan Curry. He was not the most junior officer who went with the team to Waitotara on the afternoon of 6th October, but he was the most junior, and least experienced officer, detailed to carry out the interviews.

By the time the team arrived back at Wanganui police headquarters, the police had managed to secure the services of a Mr. J.W.Abernethy as an interpreter.

This was the police's second mistake, and an illustration of how important it is to be deaf-aware of all issues surrounding sign language communication.

J.W.Abernethy was a peripatetic school teacher who knew Ivan Curry, and was able to communicate in New Zealand Sign Language. However, there is a big difference in using NZSL in an educational setting when it tends to be in a Signed Supported English format, and using NZSL in a legal setting when a Deaf person is feeling anxious because of possible criminal charges and tending to use sign language in a much more fluent and idiomatic manner to get points across.

As he was to admit later, Mr. Abernethy was not really an interpreter *per se* and had no formal training in interpreting in legal situations. In short, he was out of his depth assisting the police on this occasion.

Be as that may, Constable Kerrisk conducted the second interview of Ivan Curry at Wanganui police headquarters in two parts on the evening of 6th October. The first part lasted from 6 p.m. till 7.15 p.m., when Mr. Abernethy had to leave due to a prior engagement, returning at 9.30 p.m. The second interview was concluded at 10.44 p.m., and the second statement was admitted in writing and submitted in evidence at the trial along with the other oral admissions made by Ivan Curry whilst at Waitotara that he had struck the child in the chest.

This procedure was to cause legal argument.

Mr. Abernethy was to point out later that he had no real briefing for the correct procedures in taking a statement for subsequent use in evidence. If he had, he would never have written down a statement which Ivan Curry did not understand but copied down because he was told to do so, that the statement was a true and correct record of the interview.

It was on the basis of this statement, later admitted as evidence at a pre-trial hearing, following the conclusion of the second interview, that led to the formal charging of Ivan Curry for the murder of his nephew, Sandy Wirihana-Tawake.

Ivan Curry appeared before magistrates in Wanganui District Court on 7th October and remanded into custody pending the completion of the police investigations for the Crown. In truth, the police felt they had an open and shut case, and did not seriously bother to investigate or consider any other possible causes of the death of Sandy Wirihana-Tawake. Even when they were told of another possible cause, they did not take it seriously, not bothering even to take notes or statements from witnesses.

In Waitotara those people who knew Ivan Curry well greeted the news of his being charged with murder with widespread disbelief and scepticism. Ivan Curry was known by the clinched but very apt description as a gentle giant, a simple person with no history of violence.

Ivan Curry was to be remanded in custody for an incredible 22 months!

Much of the delay was due to legal argument over the admissibility of the statements obtained from Curry by Constable Kerrisk. During the whole of this period, the police opposed bail on the grounds that (a) he had nowhere suitable to live under bail conditions, a pretty flimsy excuse given that Curry was a simple man who would prefer to live within his own community and was unlikely to abscond; (b) that his life could be endangered if he was out on bail.

Ivan Curry was represented by a senior member of the New Zealand Criminal Bar, a Mr. M.W.H.Lance, QC (later to become a District Court judge), assisted by another experienced criminal case lawyer, Mr.C.P.Brosnahan.

Their priority was to get the statements taken down by Constable Kerrisk ruled inadmissible as evidence. Without these statements, the Crown had a weak case and in all probability no prosecution would or could be carried out at all without them.

A great deal of time therefore had to be expended both on the part of the prosecution and on the part of the defence in the preparation of expert evidence on the true extent of Ivan Curry's ability to make the admissions he was said to have made.

Even before the depositions hearing on 10th February 1989, new evidence as to a possible cause of death had come to light. This was given to a police officer who had not taken part in the original investigation, but who had been detailed to take charge of the preparation of the trial documentation, Detective Mark Sutherland. He was what the police called the administrative manager of the prosecution file.

He was approached at the end of January 1989 by Whetu Curry, wife of Ivan Curry, and her friend and mentor Lisa Duxfield. Both women asked him during a twenty-minute meeting to explain to them what the autopsy report of Sandy Wirihane-Tawake had revealed, and whether or not the injuries could have been caused by the application of life saving resuscitation methods. Detective Sutherland had been privy to Whetu Curry's original statement made on 6th October where she had told the interviewing officer that she had applied some resuscitation to Sandy Tawake, and from all indications, it was believed that Whetu Curry had applied CPR as appropriate for a child. This led him to reply to the two women that as only child CPR had been applied, it could not have caused the injuries found by the pathologist.

The need to gather together expert witnesses to challenge the validity of the two statements taken from Ivan Curry by Constable Kerrisk meant that the first pre-trial hearing could not take place before 1990. This took place in Auckland over five days before the judge appointed to hear the trial, and resulted in a 55-page judgement which ruled both statements inadmissible as evidence at the trial.

As these statements were in effect confessions by Ivan Curry that he had struck the chest of the infant, this meant that if the judgement was accepted, the prosecution would have been left with a very weak case and been forced to dismiss the case. Therefore, to save their case, the prosecution made an appeal to the Court of Appeal over one of the two statements taken from Ivan Curry, the one which was taken down in Wanganui police headquarters with the aid of Mr.J.W.Abernethy.

The Court of Appeal made a judgement immediately following legal argument on 27th March 1990 restoring the second statement as admissible evidence on the basis it was a question for a jury to consider.

This meant that the prosecution could proceed, and trial was then set for early July 1990, but before this could take place, the defence found out that Whetu Curry and Lisa Duxfield had approached Detective Mark Sutherland over a year previously with what they regarded as new evidence. This fact had not been shared with the defence, neither was the fact that it had not even been investigated.

The defence then sought to overturn the Court of Appeal decision on the grounds of new evidence without actually disclosing what all this new evidence was. It was in the interests of the defence to establish that Sandy Wirihane-Tawake had been found in a state of coma by the two women, Whetu Curry and Raeone Wirihane-Tawake, on their return from their shopping trip.

The defence's motion to reverse the Court of Appeal decision was unsuccessful, and the trial proper than commenced on 23rd July 1990 in Wanganui High Court, just over 21 months following the arrest of Ivan Curry.

The first inkling of what the defence's position was (that the cause of the death was accidental) came with the cross-examination of the Crown pathologist, Dr. Samuel Chan, from whom answers were sought as to whether the cause of death was in fact accidental and not deliberate. He was also questioned as to whether he had actually performed a full autopsy including analysis of the stomach contents of the dead infant.

The real shock for the prosecution, however, came with the testimony of Whetu Curry to the witness stand. She had not been called by the Crown but by the defence, and therefore came to the stand on 26th July, on the fourth day of the trial after the prosecution had closed its case.

In her evidence, Whetu Curry testified that she and her sister Raeone had simultaneously discovered the then apparently lifeless body of Sandy Tawake upon their return from the store. Whilst Raeone was out of the room apparently demanding of Ivan what had happened, Whetu Curry had panicked and started to apply adult CPR to the infant.

Cardiac pulmonary resuscitation (CPR) is basically applying rhythmic pressure to the chest of a distressed person to encourage resumption of breathing and heart action. The degree of pressure required depends on the patient. The application of CPR to an infant of 15 months is quite different to the degree of pressure applied to an adult. Much would depend on the knowledge and training of the person applying CPR.

In her original statement given at Waitotara School on 6th October, Whetu Curry stated that she had given Sandy mouth-to-mouth resuscitation as he lay on the bed, and pushed her fingers against his chest three or four times. She stated she did not do it very hard.

In court, however, she was asked to demonstrate with a cushion exactly what she had done to the child. With one hand open and crossed over the other open hand, she had given Sandy adult CPR by pushing and nearly falling on the child. Her action caused the cushion's air to explode outwards making a very distinct sound.

This evidence caused consternation amongst the prosecution simply because they had not known of this evidence.

The defence had purposely and quite rightly kept the evidence up their sleeves after learning of it only three weeks prior to the trial. This was in fact why they had sought to overturn the Court of Appeal's ruling.

The real question was why it had taken so long for the truth to come out.

It seemed that an older woman named Lisa Duxfield sometimes acted as mentor to Whetu Curry, giving support and advice when needed. She had learned about five days after Sandy's death that Whetu Curry had used considerable pressure that morning trying to revive the child.

At the beginning, they had not realised the implications of Mrs. Curry's actions, and as they did not know of the pathologist's report, they did not appreciate these implications.

It would seem that Whetu Curry began to worry more and more about the false statement she had given on 6th October and what it would mean for herself when or if the time came to take the witness stand at her husband's trial. If the police could arrest Ivan without evidence, what about her.

Another reason was that Whetu Curry was concerned her family would attempt to lay the blame for Sandy's death on her.

Both Mrs. Curry and Mrs. Duxfield stated during their evidence in the trial that neither had confided to the child's mother or Whetu's other sisters what Mrs. Curry had done.

They also admitted they had not specifically told Detective Mark Sutherland in January 1989 that Whetu Curry had in fact applied adult CPR to the infant, not child CPR as her deposition stated.

It was clear that Lisa Duxfield was extremely cautious in what she was prepared to say to Detective Sutherland, uncertain of what the full consequences would be for herself, and in particular, Whetu Curry, and had only asked an hypothetical question as to whether the injuries could have been caused by adult CPR.

There was nonetheless criticism of Detective Sutherland's lack of action in following up the two women's enquiry. As stated in the Police Complaints Authority report, as an experienced detective he should have questioned first himself what was the real motive for the seemingly harmless enquiry by the two women, and if he had done that thinking, he might have interrogated them more

closely as to exactly what they had come to see him for, and what was behind their enquiries.
Ivan Curry was acquitted by the jury of murdering Sandy Wirihane-Tawake, in August 1990, a full 22 months following his arrest.

II

If everyone thought that was the end of the matter, they had another think coming.
On Sunday 12 July 1992, a television documentary was broadcast on TVNZ1, called *The Remand of Ivan Curry*.
The tone of the documentary was set right from the beginning with this opening comment:

> *"This film is an account of a police investigation into the death of a child, and the resulting arrest and prosecution for murder of a man who was innocent."*

By this forthright statement as an opening comment, the film required from its audience an acceptance that Ivan Curry was innocent not because of the jury's verdict, but that he was so clearly innocent that he should never have been put on trial at all. The programme contended that the trial came about because of police rigidity and incompetence in the investigation, and a justice system that was powerless to provide a remedy.
There were several specific issues raised by the documentary:

- The deployment of Constable Kerrisk by Detective Senior Sergeant Scott to interview Ivan Curry.

- The failure of Detective Sutherland to follow up and investigate the evidence of Whetu Curry.
- Failure to have the stomach contents analysed.
- Delay and bail.
- Miscellaneous complaints about the investigation and trial, and other matters.

One of the strongest criticisms was linked with the deployment of Constable Kerrisk to interview Ivan Curry. As one of the defence lawyers was quoted in the programme:

> "What they did was to take the most junior officer they had out there, a person in the uniform branch but had recently been seconded to the C.I.B., and they directed him off to interview the most difficult person that was there to be seen. Now that was plain stupidity."

Such was the furore created by the programme, that the Minister of Police was compelled to refer the matter to the Police Complaints Authority for an investigation to take place.

The investigation was entrusted to a senior High Court judge, Mr. Justice J.F.Jeffries, who subsequently produced a 39-page report in September 1992.

Although the report found some criticism, particularly of Detective Senior Sergeant Scott's deployment of Constable Kerrisk and the failure of Detective Sutherland in being more pro-active in investigating Whetu Curry's statement, it found that *"the Police and the Crown acted properly in charging Ivan Curry as occurred.."*

It also found that there could be no valid criticism made of the police or the justice system over delay or bail.

Although the report conceded that the investigation by the Authority had revealed some deficiencies in police work, and contained a recommendation that two officers be given such counselling as believed to be appropriate, it was in fact a complete whitewash.

No mention of regret for Ivan Curry's wasted 22 months.

No mention of regret for a poor awareness of the needs of Deaf people under the justice system.

The report was termed "disappointing" by the producer of the television documentary because it did not acknowledge that Ivan Curry was entitled to compensation for his 22 months in prison.

In a statement, the producer said: "If the arrest of Ivan Curry was proper police procedure, then it makes a sad commentary on normal police practice in New Zealand."

The only good thing to come out of the Ivan Curry case was an acknowledgement of the right of Deaf people to access New Zealand Sign Language and to have proper sign language interpretation under police interrogation.

Photograph and Picture Acknowledgements

Frontspiece:

Photograph of reproduction shoe in blood re-created by author.

Chapter 3 :

Photograph of Harold Winney reproduced with permission from Magazine Design & Publishing Ltd., London
Photograph of reproduction shoe taken by author.
(The reproduction shoe was re-created by Terence O'Hara)

Chapter 4 :

Photograph of William Watkins & scene outside Winson Greenprison reproduced with permission from Birmingham City Libraries..

Chapter 5 :

All photographs of Darryl Beamish, Eric Cooke, Jillian Brewer and DI Lamb reproduced with permission from the *West Australian* newspaper archives.

Research & Bibliography

Chapter 1 : Introduction

Equality Before the Law - Deaf people's access to justice, Mary Brennan & Richard Brown, Deaf Studies Research Unit, University of Durham 1997

Chapter 2 : Guilty by Reason of Deafness

Rex vs. Governor of Stafford Prison, ex parte Emery, 2KB81, 73 JP 284, 100 LT 993, 1909.
Regina vs. Roberts, All England Law Reports 340, 1953

Chapter 3 : The Case of the Bloody Footprint

The Jackson Citizen Press, 28 February 1914
The Jackson Citizen Press, 1, 2, 5 March 1914
The Jackson Citizen Press, 19,20,21 May 1914
The Jackson Citizen Patriot, 13 March 1934
Correspondence - Jackson District Library
True Detective, Summer 1997 issue

Chapter 4 : Hanged But was he Innocent?

Birmingham Gazette, 16 & 17 March 1951
Birmingham Mail, 15, 16, & 17 March 1951
Rex vs. Watkins, Trial Transcript, 1951
Murder Most Foul, Issue No. 29 1998

Chapter 5 : A Blemish on Justice

The West Australian, 21,22,23 & 24 December 1959
The West Australian, 8 April 1961
The West Australian, 5,8,9,10,11,12,15 & 16 August 1961
The West Australian, 20,21 & 22 September 1961
The West Australian, 21 October 1961
Beamish v. R, The Court of Criminal Appeal Proceedings [W.A.R. 1962]; [W.A.R.1965]
The Sydney Sun-Herald, 25 October 1963
The Murder Book of Days, Brian Lane, Headline Publishing, London 1992
The New Murderer's Who's Who, J.H.H.Gaute & Robin Odell, Harrap, London 1979
The Beamish Case, Professor Peter Brett, Melbourne University Press, Melbourne, Australia 1966
Correspondence - Research & Information department, Western Australia House, London
Correspondence - Corr, Chambers & Westgarth, Australian Solicitors, London
Correspondence - Western Australian Deaf Society Inc., Leederville, W.Australia

Chapter 6 : The Long Arrest

The Dominion, 10 June 1990
The Press (Christchurch), 14, 15 July 1992
The Press (Christchurch), 21 August 1993
Western Leader, 16 July 1992
Otago Daily Times, 22 July 1992
various undated newspaper cuttings 1990-2
Correspondence, NZ Association for the Deaf Inc.,
Correspondence, National Foundation for the Deaf Inc.
continued on next page....

continued....

Press Release, Department of Justice, NZ, 13 July 1992
The Remand of Ivan Curry, TVNZ1 documentary, broadcast on 12 July 1992
Police Complaints Authority Report, 92-035, 4 September 1992
Regina vs. Curry, 6 CRNZ 657 1990